CHARACTERISTICS OF THE SPIRITUAL PATH

By
His Holiness POPE SHENOUDA III

© 2020 ACTS Press

All rights reserved. No part of this publication may be reproduced, distributed, or transmitted in any form or by any means, including photocopying, recording, or other electronic or mechanical methods, without the prior written permission of ACTS Press, except noncommercial uses permitted by copyright law. For permission requests, please contact ACTS Press.

St. Athanasius St. Cyril Theological School (ACTS) Press

1617 W. La Palma Ave, Anaheim, CA 92801

www.acts.press

Special discounts are available on quantity purchases by corporations, associations, and others. For details, contact ACTS Press.

Printed in the United States of America

ISBN: 978-1-940661-87-2

Contents

Preface to the Second English Edition by ACTS Press i
Introduction iii
Reasons for Success in the Spiritual Goal 1
Continuity in the Spiritual Life 13
The Fear of God 23
Self-Coercion 31
Spiritual Conduct 39
Uprightness 47
Spiritual Goals 55
Commitment 63
Wisdom and Discernment 71
Inner and Positive Work 91
Faithfulness 105
Diligence 127
Precision 133
The Victorious Life 141
Light and Darkness 149
The Life of Submission 157
The Life of Thanksgiving 165
The Narrow Path 175
The Journey Towards Growth and Perfection 183

Preface to the Second English Edition by ACTS Press

This book is a new, complete and original translation of His Holiness Pope Shenouda's Arabic book maʿālim al-ṭarīq al-rūḥy, published 1989 by Anba Rewis Press in Cairo. This edition has been reviewed and edited by ACTS Press under the leadership and guidance of His Eminence Metropolitan Serapion and His Grace Bishop Kyrillos.

The following introduction to the text was published in both the Arabic and English editions penned by His Holiness. As His Holiness writes in the introduction, the book is a compilation of lectures orally delivered over decades while H.H. was serving as General Bishop of Education and later a Patriarch of the Great City of Alexandria. As a result, it was necessary in this edition to include citations for numerous patristic, ecclesiastic, hagiographic and literary references made in the text, absent from the original Arabic version. To the extent sources for those references were found as part of this edition, footnotes have been added, without a citation to a specific edition or publication, in order to assist the reader in locating the source material.

The first English translation was published by Anba Rewis Press in 2015. That edition closely followed the structure and text of the Arabic edition and, as a result, reflected the original style of the material as orally delivered lectures. This second English edition also closely follows the text, but with an emphasis on paragraph organization for readability as a book as well as reformatting thought headings in the Arabic to Chapter subheadings.

Biblical quotations for the Old Testament are taken from the Orthodox Study Bible for the Old Testament and the NKJV for the New Testament, unless otherwise noted in the citation reference.

Characteristics of the Spirital Path

This book is not simply one book about the spiritual life. It contains a summary of the major essential aspects of the Orthodox Christian life with God. As such, it is essential reading for all. May God reward all the servants who diligently labored for this new edition to reach completion.

May the Lord guide you on your spiritual path to the Kingdom of the Son of His Love (Col. 1:13).

Bishop Kyrillos

October 2020

Introduction

From among the various lectures His Holiness Pope Shenouda III delivered at Saint Mark's Cathedral at Anba Reweis during the 1960s and 70s, this collection was compiled in order to explain to you the spiritual path, its signs and characteristics, and how you can walk through it.

We should first ask, what is a sound spiritual goal and how can you remain steadfast in it? Next, how can you begin and continue to persevere?

We will discuss how to begin and demonstrate that the fear of God is "the beginning" according to the Holy Bible (Prov. 9:10). The fear of God prompts you to walk through the right path, even if initially by coercion, until you reach a love of spirituality and a love for God.

We will then present the positive and inner work.

Later, we address the importance of wisdom and discernment because wisdom should permeate every spiritual endeavor.

Finally, we introduce general guidelines necessary for our spiritual endeavor—these include seriousness, commitment, meticulousness, and faithfulness in our relationship with God. Faithfulness begins by being faithful over the few things in our possession so that God may commend to us many.

All these are conducive to a victorious life since one cannot prevail in spiritual struggle without detachment from all environment devoid of spiritual enrichment. Chapter 15 below discuss the separation of light from darkness.

When someone reaches the summit of spiritual practice, he will attain complete submission to God in a life of ceaseless thanksgiving. In addition, as the Lord of Glory Himself mentioned in the Sermon on the Mount, one must enter through the narrow gate (Matt.7:13).

Where does the spiritual path lead us? The spiritual path is a journey towards perfection, attained through constant spiritual growth. Towards the end of this book we discuss spiritual growth and some of its hindrances.

Unfortunately, we cannot explain everything related to the characteristics of the spiritual path—to speak about them is to speak about the spiritual life in its fullness.

Shenouda III

CHAPTER 1

Reasons for Success in the Spiritual Goal

My friend, you are walking the path of life, and I would like to discuss with you a plan for your journey. Perhaps the first question we may come across this: what are the reasons for the success of many? There are numerous reasons.

First, those who have succeeded in the spiritual life had clear, strong goals set before them. And they used all their effort to accomplish those goals. Their appreciation of goal and desire to accomplish it gave them enthusiasm, strength, diligence and motivation. It also gave them focus and discipline in their lives. Thus, their entire capability, effort, and action aligned into one direction, without any deviation. Each goal gave value to their life, and reason for existence. Life became delightful and purposeful with there goals. Each minute of their life became valuable. The more sublime and elevated the goal, the greater the value of life became, and the more fervently the fire burned inside there hearts to achieve it.

On the other hand, those who live without a goal suffer from a monotonous life that is too heavy to bear. Their life is meaningless and tasteless, wavering and without direction. They are restless and hesitant in all their ways. They suffer from boredom and detachment, feeling that their life is worthless, pointless, and trivial. They frequently search for means to pass the time because time has neither a value nor meaning to them. They often ask: "Why are we alive? Why did God create us? What is the meaning of life? What is its aim and purpose?" How pitiable are poor people! They live and do not know why! They are sucked in along the whirlpool of life without any true awareness. And if they become aware, they ask: "Where are we going?" If only they would find a purpose for their life, all these questions would vanish.

Here, we turn to the goals that guide people in life. And the goal itself defines the means of achieving it. Some aim for wealth, positions, titles, authority, possessions or success at work. Others focus on pleasure—whether pleasure of the senses, eating and drinking, pleasures of the flesh, or comfort. Still others aim to marry and settle or to succeed in their studies.

We cannot call all of these goals. Rather, they are desires and pleasures. Even if we were to consider them goals, they would be temporary, transient and superficial goals that lack depth and are limited by time. The Lord summaries all this in his words to Martha: "you are worried and troubled about many things. But one thing is needed" (Luke 10:41-42).

❊ The Sole Goal is God ❊

A spiritual person's sole goal is God. His only aim is to grow closer to God, to know Him, to love Him, and to live with Him. God abides in his heart and he abides in the heart of God. He lovingly says to God, "What do I desire on earth besides You?" (Psalm 72:25). Thus, by clinging to God he can do without all things. His love for God leads him to temperance and asceticism. The more he experiences and tastes the sweetness of life with God, the more he feels that everything in the world is vanity and grasping for the wind (Ecc. 2:11). As mentioned in Proverbs, "A satisfied soul mocks the honeycomb" (Proverbs 27:7). In the same manner, a soul that is satisfied by God loathes all the pleasures of the world.

❊ False Aims ❊

Contentment displeases the devil who wanders about the earth disseminating various desires. He sows and cultivates seeds of aspiration and desire to deceive man into losing the spiritual aim of abiding in God and preparing for eternal life. The devil overwhelms worldly people with a flood of desires that can never be satisfied. For, deep inside every person is a desire for the Infinite, and everything in the world is finite.

The first goal presented by the devil is the self. The self becomes an idol that man worships—the focus and center of all his thoughts. Man seeks how to edify it, build it, magnify it, and make it the object of people's love and praise. The devil makes man so preoccupied with the self that he is willing to forgo everything else for its sake, even his relationship with God.

Competition arises between the self and God. The ego first enters the heart and shares it with God, but gradually, it takes over and becomes its exclusive owner. In turning to worship the self, man continues to think daily: "What am I going to be? When am I going to be? How shall I be? And how shall I develop into something bigger and greater?"

However, if he would be concerned about his self in a spiritual manner, he would sacrifice it for the sake of God and others. Thus, he would live a life of sacrificial love that gives itself as a ransom for others. Only then would he discover his true self. This legitimate discovery of the self amounts to holiness, righteousness, and perfection, which is the discovery of God, Himself.

St. Paul the Apostle says about life with God, "Nor do I count my life dear to myself..." (Acts 20:24). Thus, he who gives consideration to his self entangles it with the pleasures of the world and, consequently, makes them his aim. He preoccupies himself with the glamour of the present world, its glory, pleasures, amusements, dreams and aspirations such that he does not think of his eternity. He remains intoxicated by worldly passions and only becomes sober at the hour of his death as he leaves the world against his will.

As for you: do not think in this manner or walk in this direction. Rather, regard every goal that snatches you from God and your salvation as a trick from the devil. So, firmly renounce it! In like manner, reject every instrument that keeps you away from your spiritual aim. Do not allow your ego to compete with God. And do not let the world become a desire for you. As the Holy Bible says, "the world is passing away, and the lust of it" (1 John 2:17) and "friendship with the world is enmity with God" (James 4:4). Therefore, reconsider all your goals and means for achieving them in the light of your eternal life and spiritual aim which is the love of God.

Every aim against the kingdom of God is a deviation from the spiritual path. Relinquish anything that conflicts with the love of God in your heart, however great its value may be. Then, say to the Lord with Saint Peter the Apostle, "we have left all and followed You" (Matt. 19:27).

The chaste Joseph lost his freedom when he was sold as a slave. He lost his reputation when he was thrown into prison. He lost his parents, his brothers, and his homeland. But God alone was sufficient for him. God was his aim. Whoever's aim is God is not at a loss when he forgoes any worldly matter.

Because God was the sole aim of Abraham, the father of the patriarchs, it was easy for him to leave his entire family, kindred and country (Gen. 12:1), to be estranged, not knowing where he was going (Heb. 11:8), and even to take his only son and offer him as a burnt offering to the Lord.

It was easy for Saint Paul the Apostle to renounce his position and authority since neither was his aim. He was able to say: "I have suffered the loss of all things, and count them as rubbish, that I may gain Christ" (Phil. 3:8). Christ was the goal for which he was glad to sacrifice all other things.

Daniel the Prophet did not care for the royal palace, high ranks, or the king's delicacies. He did not even care about his life when he was thrown into the lions' den because he had a sole aim, before which all else diminished.

He whose goal is God does not deem even spiritual matters his goal! Some have made prayer their goal such that he prays, not out of love for God, but because he wants to become a man of prayer! He studies theology as an aim, not in order to know God and abide in Him, but in order to become a theologian, acquire fame, and attain a high position! Likewise, fasting and every other spiritual endeavor can be transformed into an aim in and of itself if man practices it either for his own self-satisfaction or to please other people!

Spiritual practices are means, not goals. Prayer, fasting, knowledge, contemplation and reading are means that lead you to your sole aim, which is God, loving and abiding in Him. If you turn these practices into aims, then you have pursued them as ends in themselves. You may advance in them while remaining far from God who said, "These people honor Me with their lips, but their heart is far from Me" (Matt. 15:8).

Even monasticism and consecration should not be turned into aims. Monasticism is merely a path that leads to God, it is a detachment from all in order to be attached to One, God alone. If monasticism turns into a goal, then solitude and silence become aims in themselves, and how easily can the commandments of God be broken for the sake of those aims! A monk could desert his monastery in search of the life of solitude. He could live like a hermit, but would, nevertheless, lack the true virtues of solitude and the opportunity to grow closer in the love of God. As Isaac the Syrian says, "There is a person who stays fifty years in a cell and does not know how to stay in his cell."

Some people may transform reform into a goal. For the sake of reform, they rebel, contend, judge and defame people. They forsake their love for others. They lose their serenity and peace. They revile and curse; they become enraged and furious, and turn into an exploding bomb scattering sharp fragments everywhere. If you search for their relationship with God, you will not find it. They transformed reform into an irreligious zeal, deprived of God and void of love.

The same happens with service. Many embark on the path of service to glorify God, only to end up with self-arrogance and self-glory. They start with God as their aim, then they put the service beside Him, sometimes even before Him, until it becomes their single aim. Pursuit of a successful service turns into a pursuit of personal success. Service becomes a source of attention and authority, a social activity and an outlet of energy, far from God. They focus on their own intelligence, cleverness, and craftiness. The spiritual aim, however, which should be God, is lost!

But as for you, in every spiritual work, say with David the Prophet, "I have set the Lord always before me" (Psalm 15:8). Let God be your sole goal, and serve only for His sake. If the service clashes with God, leave it! For it is easy for the devil to mislead you, even inside the Church. Remember that the elder brother of the prodigal son was far from the love of his father even while serving him, as he said, "these many years…" (Luke. 15:25-32).

So, God asks you: "Where am I amidst your aims?" Reply to this question in all honesty. Is God one of your goals? Is He your primary goal? Is He your sole aim? Or, is He not an aim at all? Do you put Him at the end of your list such that you sometimes remember Him and sometimes do not? Has God become only a means to achieve your goals? And if He does not fulfil them for you, you become angry and cut off your relationship with Him?

Do you love God as He loves you? Have you given your whole heart to Him? Are there other aims besides Him competing to be the primary goal? Are you mindful of your eternity and seek to reach the bosom of God? Your goal will dictate your life and the means by which you live it. Examine yourself.

❊ The Constancy of the Spiritual Goal ❊

The spiritual person is consistent in his goal and means. He has a clear, unshakeable and unchangeable vision. His mind is focused on the goal, pursuing it with all his effort and desire. He does not deviate from it. All his ways lead to it, like the needle of a compass leads to the same direction, whichever way the compass is moved. He is a stable, steadfast and resolute, unaffected by the vagaries of life and the changes of the outside world.

The spiritual poet has rightly spoken of the true man that "he advances without changing, grows without becoming haughty, and remains steady in his strides." The weak person, however, is shaken. His experiences, disappointment, affliction, trial, tribulation and other circumstances cause him to waver and drift from his path. He is tempted by desire, fear and new thoughts that cross his paths.

Thus, many have started in the Spirit and then completed their path in the flesh. They started with God and ended with the world. We all know people who seemed to have a spiritual goal but neither they nor their goal longer exist! The whirlwind of this world engulfed them along with their spirituality. This phenomenon is not exclusive to our generation. The Holy Bible presents us with various examples of individuals who started but did not continue—those whose aim deviated along the way.

❊ Examples of Those who Fell ❊

One of these examples is Demas, the disciple of Saint Paul the Apostle, of whom he said, "Demas has forsaken me, having loved this present world" (2 Tim. 4:10). What happened to Demas happened to many others of whom the Apostle Paul said in his Epistle to the Philippians, "For many walk, of whom I have told you often, and now tell you even weeping, that they are the enemies of the cross of Christ: whose end is destruction, whose god is their belly, and whose glory is their shame - who set their mind on earthly things" (Phil. 3:18,19). All of these people were friends of the great Apostle and had a glorious past in the ministry. They lived for their spiritual goal but abandoned it when other desires infiltrated their hearts and ruled over them. Perhaps, they tried to wed both God and the world, living with Sarah and Hagar in the same house like Abraham, loving God and the green lands of Sodom like the righteous Lot.

Samson began his life consecrated to God and the Spirit of the Lord was moving him (Judges 13:25). Then what happened?

Desire entered the heart of Samson instead of God, so the Lord departed from him (Judges 16:20). Therefore, it is not enough to have the Lord as your goal. You must also commit to this goal above all so that no other lust enters your heart. For you cannot bring together your oath and Delilah, however wise you may think you are.

Solomon, the wisest on earth, gives us an example. He undoubtedly started with a spiritual aim. God appeared to him twice and endowed him with wisdom. Nevertheless, he wanted to compromise between God and the pleasures of the world. He failed, lost his spiritual aim and fell (1 Kings 11). Solomon the Wise fell? What a catastrophe! This is the consequence of abandoning your goal or exchanging it for another desire. But he who adheres to his goal finds himself walking steadfastly towards God.

Contemplate on the waters of the Flood and learn from them. They covered the whole earth, even the tops of the high mountains, yet the Ark was not affected in the least, rather it sailed on top because its aim was God. God was undoubtedly inside the Ark, protecting and directing it. Truly, a sound aim gives life, energy and an ability to walk toward God. It also gives power to withstand adverse currents. A person with a strong goal is not dragged by any adverse tide because his will is fixed on his aim. A small fish can withstand the tide's current and continue along its way because it has a life and a will moving it, whereas a large plank of wood is pushed and pulled to wherever the current takes it because it has no life and no aim.

The children of Israel left the slavery of Pharaoh, having been saved from destruction, and crossed the Red Sea. They had a good start, but the lack of a persistent, spiritual aim led to their downfall in the wilderness of Sinai. They were fed manna and quail and were shaded by the cloud of God. But with their own selves as the aim, they murmured and complained against God. They physically left the slavery of Pharaoh but were not able to escape the bonds of internal slavery and so, they perished. It was Moses, not the Israelites, who had the right goal. All the ritualistic worship they exercised did not help them follow the path of Moses. It is indeed very easy for a heart that is not truly and fully in the hands of God to break every covenant it makes with Him and stray away from its goals toward other distractions.

Likewise, Lot's wife left Sodom, yet her heart remained there. Her departure from the land of sin was not from the heart nor for the sake of God. Her hand held on to the angel guiding her and her family, while her heart was burning with desire for the things inside the burning city. It is strange that she did not perish inside Sodom, but rather after she left it! She turned into a pillar of salt. Her death became salt to the world, that is, a spiritual lesson about the danger of looking back.

A person who has a true, constant aim clings to God and never looks back, lest he be rebuked by the words of Elijah, "How long will you falter between two opinions? If the Lord is God, follow Him, but if Baal, then follow him" (1 Kings 18:21). If your aim is God, do not have two hearts and do not falter.

This was Judas' problem. He sat with the Lord Christ at the same table, ate with Him from the same dish, yet plotted against Him with the elders and leaders of the Jews. He was a disciple of the Lord but had no goal. He kissed the Lord, but delivered Him to His enemies. His aimless life became a burden to him and everyone else and so, he perished.

After Nicodemus met the Lord and experienced Him, he was no longer able to remain His companion and a member of the Sanhedrin at the same time.

Ananias and Sapphira wanted to unlawfully keep some of their money while appearing before the people as pious servants who placed all their money at the feet of the Apostles. At the end, they died having profited neither the money nor membership in the Church. Their goal faltered between their two different desires. Their example is similar to that of Pilate, who wanted to appease his conscience and simultaneously please the Jews. When he failed, he cleansed his hands with water but could not cleanse his heart.

The rich young man also wanted to combine two aims. When the Lord, the Examiner of hearts, revealed the young man's real self, he went away sorrowful. He was seeking to attain eternal life, having kept the commandments from his youth, but his heart loved the present world (Matt. 19:16-22). When the Lord revealed to him his frailty and called him to have one aim and give up all others, he went away sorrowful. Likewise, all those who try to place other aims next to God will go away sorrowful. Many claim that their goal is God yet seek to enter by the wide gate that does not lead to Him even though "we must through many tribulations enter the kingdom of God" (Acts 14:22).

Those who make God their aim ought to suffer for His sake, sacrificing themselves for Him, knowing that their labor in the Lord is not in vain, as the Holy Bible says, "each one will receive his own reward according to his own labor" (1 Cor. 3:8). Those people remain steadfast in their spiritual goal and do not change it. They choose God as their goal, without regret, hesitation, reconsideration or looking back. They do not question the matter. They leave no room for negotiation with the devil. Their path is clear and fixed before them. They firmly settled the matter long ago, as the Apostle Saint Paul said, "Therefore, my beloved brethren, be steadfast, immovable, always abounding in the work of the Lord, knowing that your labor is not in vain in the Lord" (1 Cor. 15:58). These people do not live a life of conflict between good and evil or between God and the world. Conflict signifies instability. Yet, their path in life is straight, steadfast and invariable. Their hearts are full of God's love. They possess no other pleasures that conflict with their love for God; He is their sole longing and desire, filling their hearts with His overflowing love.

❈ Examples of Steadfastness ❈

Let us now explore some examples to illustrate the spiritual lessons of steadfastness.

The Repentant

The stories of steadfast individuals provide insight into a life of commitment to one's spiritual aim. These people abandoned sin for good and did not return to it. Saint Augustine did not return to his former life of sin after his repentance, nor did Saint Moses the Black, Saint Mary of Egypt or Saint Pelagia. Once God became their aim, their life was transformed, without any relapse or regression. They uprooted sin from their hearts and turned to God Whom they chose with amazing sincerity and utter devotion. They can be likened to a surgeon who performs surgery to remove a tumor. He does not leave any portion of it behind or else the tumor returns in a worse state.

For this reason, whoever claims that he has repented yet continues to fall and arise repeatedly is not focused on his aim and has not experienced true repentance. A poet described this state saying: "When can a building be complete, if you build up but another tears down?" Repentance is not a temporary hiatus from sin for man to return to it at a later time. Rather, it is the permanent elimination of all bonds of sin, along with any attachment or love for it.

One of the saints defined repentance as, "exchanging one desire for another," meaning the replacement of worldly desires with the desire for a life with God. Those sinners did not only become penitents, but saints! They walked with such steadfast resolve that they applied the words of the Lord, "And if your right eye causes you to sin, pluck it out and cast it from you; for it is more profitable for you that one of your members perish than for your whole body to be cast into hell" (Matt. 5:29-30).

The Martyrs

Another example of constancy in the spiritual aim is the lives of the martyrs. Their sole aim was God and their life with Him in eternity. That is the reason for which they followed Him wholeheartedly, even to death, not giving heed to temptation or torture. Their hearts were immovable, abiding in their Lord and Savior. As Saint Paul the Apostle said, "Who shall separate us from the love of Christ? ...For I am persuaded that neither death nor life ... nor things present nor things to come, nor height nor depth, nor any other created thing, shall be able to separate us from the love of God which is in Christ Jesus our Lord" (Rom. 8:35-39).

The Divine Calling

Commitment and constancy in the spiritual aim can also be a result of divine calling. When the Lord called Abraham the Patriarch to leave his tribe, land and father's house, he did not hesitate, but "went out, not knowing where he was going" (Heb. 11:8). Neither the promised land nor the tribe was his goal; it was God for Whose sake he left everything. Even when the Lord asked him to offer his only son as a sacrifice, he did not ponder on or debate the matter. Neither did he face an internal dilemma. Instead, he rose early in the morning and took his son, together with the wood, the knife and the fire. For Abraham, even a son was not the goal, God was.

Saint Paul the Apostle experienced a similar condition as he said: "But when it pleased God who separated me from my mother's womb and called me through His grace, to reveal His Son in me, that I might preach Him among the Gentiles, I did not immediately confer with flesh and blood, nor did I go up to Jerusalem to those who were apostles before me" (Gal. 1:15-17).

Spiritual goals demand persistence. For if the devil finds in us an indecisive and infirm will in our relationship with God, he will snatch us in his grasp and crush us like a flimsy reed.

Let us be steadfast in our love to God. Let us not have any other goal besides Him.

To Him be the glory now and forever. Amen.

CHAPTER 2

Continuity in the Spiritual Life

It is essential to start walking the spiritual path and to begin a relationship with God. Many have not yet started and are estranged from God. They live a secular life, absorbed in material matters, the desires of the flesh, and the various responsibilities of life. They have not yet discovered their way to spirituality. Instead, they live in a labyrinth, a vortex where the thought of their eternal life has not once crossed their minds. If only they begin to care for their eternal life, they will experience a fundamental transformation of their lives.

The motives to begin this journey are many, and differ from one person to another. One person may be touched by a sermon; another by a tragic event, like the illness or death of a loved one; and another by the works of grace awakening the conscience and directing it back towards God. It could also be the decision of a spiritual person during a certain occasion, like New Years, to commit to a relationship with God and take an active step towards building a relationship with Him.

Beginning in the spiritual life can also be the result of God's grace. During this period, the person may experience strong zeal, spiritual fervor, and determination. This period of grace may continue for several days. This period may be prolonged, but then the person either becomes lukewarm, or reverts back to his former state and ceases to continue on his path; his former love grows cold (Rev. 2:4).

Therefore, it is important to not only begin but all the more to continue.

❈ Continuity ❈

Many people repent, confess, take communion and start to sense an excellent spiritual state with a fresh life of repentance, full of vigor and enthusiasm. However, after a few days, they return to their former state prior to repentance. Their problem is lack of continuity in the life of repentance. Indeed, it is easy to live a life of holiness for a single day! A person may start an ascetic spiritual practice, such as the practice of silence to evade the errors of the tongue, and commit to it for a day or two, but then abandon silence and this spiritual exercise. Thus, it is beneficial to begin, but more so to continue.

Take Saint Peter the Apostle as an example. At one point, he was full of zeal for the Lord and said to Him, "Even if all are made to stumble because of You, I will never be made to stumble" (Matt. 26:33). Beautiful words! He indeed walked with the Lord and was zealous to the extent of cutting off the ear of the servant (Matt. 26:51). But his zeal did not continue. He fell, denied the Lord, and began to curse, saying: "I do not know the Man!" (Matt. 26:74).

Another example is the person who vows. He may make a vow with all emotion, being utterly ready to commit to it. But he soon rethinks it and may delay in performing the vow, feel that it is too burdensome to fulfill or, or negotiate in altering it!

In like manner are those who make covenants with God. This is common at the beginning of spiritual zeal, of repentance, or an ascetic practice. Yet, this zeal does not continue. There are many who made covenants beyond their capabilities such as taking a vow of celibacy or monasticism, or others who took a pledge that they will not remarry after the death of their spouse. Their zeal dissipated. It would have been better to offer these to God as prayers and desires, rather than vows.

We often err when we say, "God accepted the repentance of Augustine, Moses the Black, Mary of Egypt, and Pelagia!" It is true that God accepted their repentance, but their repentance did not lead to a return to sin. These saints continued in their repentance and advanced every day upwards on the ladder of virtue.

Likewise, in service, many began and did not continue. Many were once great in their service, but later vanished as they became preoccupied by the world and its affairs. Their mind was overwhelmed by their position, family, wealth, and education, and they abandoned the Divine service. That is why the Apostle Saint Paul advises servants to "be steadfast, immovable, always abounding in the work of the Lord, knowing that your labor is not in vain in the Lord" (1 Cor. 15:58).

What applies for service also applies for repentance. Many fervently repented with tears and took vows, they had a good start to their relationship with God, but it did not last. They reverted once again to their former state and forgot their initial feelings. But the repentance of the great saints such as Augustine, Moses the Black, Pelagia, and Mary of Egypt, was a point of transformation in their lives at which they turned to a life of purity, advancing in the life of holiness and walking in the path of perfection.

❈ The Outcome of Your Conduct ❈

The Holy Bible tells us concerning the saints: "whose faith follow, considering the outcome of their conduct" (Heb. 13:7). What mattered then is the outcome of their conduct and not its beginning. This is the reason why, in the Synaxarium, we celebrate the day of their departure or martyrdom. Similarly, in the Commemoration of the Saints during the Divine Liturgy, we mention all those who "were perfected in the faith."

Demas, at the beginning of his ministry, was one of the pillars of the Church whom Saint Paul the Apostle mentioned along with his saintly assistants Mark, Luke, and Aristarchus (Phil. 1:24). But, Demas did not continue in this conduct. He did not complete his service; and his life ended in a sorrowful manner. The Apostle Paul said, "Demas has forsaken me, having loved this present world" (2 Tim.4:10). This was not only true in the case of Demas. But many others who started serving with Saint Paul, and were even praised by him, did not continue. The Apostle finally said about them: "For many walk, of whom I have told you often, and now tell you even weeping, that they are the enemies of the cross of Christ: whose end is destruction, whose god is their belly, and whose glory is in their shame - who set their mind on earthly things" (Phil. 3:18,19).

Therefore, do not boast about your beginning, rather strive to continue so that you may attain perfection. Do not start your journey with God and hasten to tell everyone that you are saved, forgetting that you ought to complete your life in faith, heeding the words of the Apostle, "work out your own salvation with fear and trembling" (Phil. 2:12).

Obtaining the grace of salvation through faith and baptism does not negate the fact that there is a long path before you along which you must continue to walk diligently in repentance and with good deeds, participating in the Holy Mysteries and all the means of grace. So put before you the words of Saint Paul: "Let him who thinks he stands take heed lest he fall" (1 Cor. 10:12) and: "Do not be haughty but fear" (Romans 11:20). Therefore, be humble because the Holy Bible says that sin "has cast down many wounded, and all who were slain by her were strong men" (Prov. 7:26). Saint Peter also says, "Be sober, be vigilant; because your adversary the devil walks about like a roaring lion, seeking whom he may devour" (1 Peter 5:8).

You should continue walking your path so that you may be saved on the Day of the Lord. Remember that the Apostle Paul rebuked the Galatians saying, "Having begun in the Spirit, are you now being made perfect by the flesh?" (Gal. 3:3). Therefore, you must begin and continue on your spiritual path with the Spirit, not the flesh.

❦ Spiritual Warfare ❦

It is not sufficient to only take one step along the spiritual path, because one step does not lead you to the goal. Neither does it give you experience in the spiritual life. Rather, you must experience the devils' combats, tricks, and deceptions.

God often does not allow the devil to wage his wars against you at the beginning of your path, lest you despair. However, if God does allow the devil to tempt you, in order to test the sincerity of your intentions, He makes the warfare very light because He takes compassion on the weakness of beginners. The more a person progresses in his spiritual path, the more intense the envy of the devils and their warfare becomes. Nevertheless, God's grace abounds towards the believer to support him in his struggle and shield him from the devils' attacks.

The path of the spiritual life helps a person acquire humility and experience. The more a person experiences the intense warfare of the enemy, the more he recognizes his weakness and humbles himself. He falls and rises again, training himself in the prayers that raise him up. He also feels compassion for those who fall. He learns to patiently endure, remaining steadfast in his spiritual path despite all the obstacles of the enemy. He remembers the words of the Lord Christ to His disciples, "You are those who have continued with Me in My trials" (Luke 22:28). Yes, they continued. They were like the house that was built on the rock. The wind blew and the heavy rain poured. But, neither could not bring it down. It was a strong house. Its strength was the result of its firm foundation on the rock, unlike the house built on sand which, having no foundation, could not stand and fell. Another example is the plant which has no root and withers away (Matt. 13:6).

❦ Rooted in Christ ❦

A person who begins the spiritual path and grows for a while but later withdraws and abandons it is not rooted in Christ. He is like a plant that sprouts on the face of the earth, but quickly dries up because it has no roots.

What is the meaning of "having no root?" Often, a person approaches spiritual life as a result of a particular incident, tragic event, sermon, book, or problem in which he said to God, "If You deliver me, I will live my entire life for You." God delivers him, so he follows Him for a little while, but having no root, he withers away.

What then is the root? The root is a life of profound faith and true love. It is a personal relationship with God, communion with Him, and knowledge of Him. It is not merely a series of external rituals that do not spring from the heart. A person whose life is merely a set of practices void of love will not be able to persevere.

A young lady, for example, can hear a sermon about modest and appropriate dress and adornments. She may feel moved and may start to change her outward appearance. However, she remains unchanged within; the love of God has not yet entered her heart to change it. True prudence, asceticism, and pursuit of eternal life are not established in her inner self. As a result, her decent outward appearance is temporary, and she is unable to maintain it. Having no root, she withers away.

Another example is a youth who decides to cut his long hair as an ascetic practice for the New Year. If he is not convinced of the triviality of outward appearances and of the need to base his character on sound foundations, this young man will soon leave his hair to grow again, unable to find a justification to cut it. He will always await the beginning of another year or another spiritual occasion to make a change.

Religiosity for such persons is reserved for occasions. It has no strong foundation and does not spring from the heart, rather it is transitory and quick to vanish. It is like the house built on sand, having no foundation, it collapses.

Therefore, in order for a person to remain steadfast, he must have a spiritual foundation firmly rooted and fixed in his heart. Spirituality neither begins nor abounds as a result of obedience to parents, spiritual guides, or leaders. Rather, it requires developing a relationship with God, one that starts from the heart. It is based on faith in the spiritual and eternal life and profound love for God, without superficial displays and shallow practices. It thus begins with correcting the inner self.

❋ Correcting the Inner Self ❋

A person who frequently gets angry and enraged, raising his voice, losing his temper, and mistreating others may tell himself remorsefully, "I have to train myself to abandon anger." Even though he actually starts to train himself, he is unable to continue because he has no root.

How then can he get rid of his anger?

He must search within him for the source of this sin and treat it. What triggers his anger may be his pride; his inability to face disapproval, opposition, redirection, or criticism. It could be his love of dignity and praise, or even a desire to enforce his own opinion and interests regardless of others. Anger can also be caused by hatred towards a certain person. Whatever the reason may be, one needs to treat the root cause first. Only then, will he be able to succeed in his practices.

We must treat the causes and not just the symptoms. Do you treat a patient suffering from a high body temperature with ice or aspirin? Would you not first search for the cause of this rise in temperature then treat it? It could be a case of tonsillitis, an inflammation in another part of the body, or a fever. Thus, effective treatments need proper examination.

Do not correct your symptoms, meaning do not correct your external behavior, without treating the cause. The heart within must be changed, and to do that, you must rectify the sources from which sin springs. Your repentance and spiritual endeavors can then succeed because they will be firmly rooted inside your heart. Thus, the Lord said to the angel of the church of Ephesus, "Remember therefore, from where you have fallen; repent..." (Rev. 2:5).

When the righteous fall, they quickly rise again. David fell, but he rose with strength because his roots were firm. Peter denied Christ, but he wept bitterly and repented because his heart was rooted in the love of the Lord (John 21:16). The mistakes of those saints were accidental, their heart within remained pure. Thus, we can say that their falls were sins of weakness and not sins of betrayal to the Lord. That was the essential difference between Peter's sin and Judas's sin. Peter sinned due to weakness, but Judas sinned due to betrayal. He who sins because of weakness rises quickly as is written, "For righteous men may fall seven times and rise again" (Prov. 24:16).

A person's love for God moves him to repent and continue in repentance. While his love for sin makes him repeatedly return to it, regardless of any repentance. Continuity, therefore, depends on the inclinations of your heart and the direction it chooses to follow. A heart full of love for God is what causes the righteous to rise up no matter how many times they fall, it makes them "renew their strength, they shall mount up with wings like eagles, they shall run and not be weary, they shall walk and not faint" (Isa. 40:31).

Deepen your roots in life with God. Extend them deeper underground before growing out trunks and branches above. Remember that the foundation and support of any growth is the root.

A novice in monasticism, for example, may plead with his father of confession to allow him to fast long hours in addition to hundreds of prostrations and a strict practice of solitude and silence. However, his spiritual father says to him, "Wait, my son, until we give consideration to the inner self first. Let us lay a foundation of true love for God, humility, meekness, gentleness, and kindness in dealing with people. Then we will build on this foundation."

Therefore, start building your life from within first, caring for depth more so than height, and purifying your intentions, more than outward appearances. It is not enough to abandon sin; you must find and eradicate its causes, so you do not fall into it once more. In this manner, you will be able to continue in your repentance. The Lord Jesus Christ said, "Remember therefore from where you have fallen; repent" (Rev. 2:5). Uproot the thorns which surround you so that your plant may be able to grow without choking. Delve into the depths of your inner self, cleanse and correct what lies there.

Many begin their spiritual life by self-coercion, suppressing their will and forcing the soul to walk in the spiritual path. We do not oppose this as it is a type of necessary spiritual striving. But why by force? Because there is no love. You force yourself to practice a virtue because the love of that virtue is not in your heart. If you attain that love, self-coercion will disappear. You will start to seek and practice a virtue naturally, walking in it without fear of falling.

This foundation of love is what we want to establish in our hearts. If a car's motor is functioning, it can start by itself and does not need its owner to push it. Its inside—the motor—moves it. My advice to you is to care for your inward self in order to be able to live a consistent spiritual life. If you cannot attain the love of God, place God's fear before your eyes and say as Elijah used to say, "the Lord of hosts lives, before Whom I stand" (1 Kings 18:15). Whenever you are tempted to sin, say to yourself as Joseph the Righteous said, "How then can I do this great wickedness, and sin against God?" (Gen. 39:9).

Do not let your spiritual life depend on a series of occasions. When there is a festive week in the church, your spirit is revived, but then weakens afterwards. On New Year's Eve or after attending the Divine Liturgy on one of the Lord's Feasts, your spirituality rises but then falls afterwards. Do not let your spirit walk aimlessly without a spiritual plan, for it is not fitting that it be so. Have your inner faith and life with God be your motivation each day and at every hour.

CHAPTER 3

The Fear of God

We thank God who imparted to us the knowledge of the spiritual path that leads us to Him. By laying down the sequential steps and the characteristics of the path, He leads us to the sole goal - God. What then is the starting point of the spiritual path? It is the fear of God as mentioned twice in the Holy Scriptures, "The fear of the Lord is the beginning of wisdom" (Prov. 9:10; Ps. 111:10).

❃ The Love of God and the Fear of God ❃

Discourse about the fear of God may not be appealing to some people who are more accustomed to hearing about the love of God. However, the love of God does not at all contradict the fear of God, for it is a higher status that surpasses, yet guards, it. It can be likened to a university student who still employs the basics of reading, writing, and mathematics in his studies.

Those who avoid the fear of God make their pretext the words of Saint John the Apostle, "There is no fear in love; but perfect love casts out fear" (1 John 4:18). To reply to them we say: Who of us has reached this perfect love, the love with which you love God with all your heart, with all your soul, and with all your might (Deut. 6:5; Matt. 22:37)? Have you acquired this level of love which reigns over all your feelings to the extent that you no longer love anything in the world? Are you confident that "friendship with the world is enmity with God" (James 4:4) and that "If anyone loves the world, the love of the Father is not in him" (1 John 2:15)? Have you reached this level? Have you reached the Divine love which makes you pray continually and not lose heart (Lk.18:1)? Do you pray with all your heart, in deep love and contemplation?!

If you have reached this level, you will not fear because your perfect love for God will cast out fear. But if you have not yet reached perfect love, do not claim that you possess it and do not attribute its spiritual outcomes to your own spiritual level. If you still fall into sin and are sometimes alienated from God, do not attribute perfect love to yourself. If you grow lukewarm in spiritual matters and are not profound in your prayers and contemplations, you have undoubtedly not yet reached perfect love. Thus, it would be very beneficial for you to live in the fear of God.

Be confident that the fear of God is the path that leads you to His love. If you fear God, you will be afraid to sin lest you be subject to His correction and wrath. You will be afraid to fall because sin separates you from God and His angels. It separates you from the Kingdom and the saints. That is why the fear of God pushes you to keep His commandments. When you walk in the path of God, you will feel the pleasure of the spiritual life and will rejoice in His commandments as one who finds great treasure (Psa. 118:162). You will be glad when others say to you: "Let us go into the house of the Lord" and will rejoice in the Lord saying: "Oh, how I love Your law! It is my meditation all day" (Ps. 118:97).

Thus, one progressively moves from the fear of God to the love of God. When you grow in the love of God and reach perfect love, fear vanishes. God formed our nature and knows our weakness and tendency to fall. He also knows the power of our adversary, the devil, who walks about like a roaring lion, seeking whom he may devour (1 Peter 5:8). For this reason, God, knowing the great spiritual benefits inherent in fear, endows us with this virtue so that we may benefit from it and gradually advance towards love in a natural and simple way.

❧ Spiritual Benefits from the Fear of God ❧

What, then, are the spiritual benefits of the fear of God?

Foremost, the fear of God is a shield against falling. The fear of

God restrains us from committing sin, and if we do fall, it becomes our impetus to repent.

We say this because many jump straight to the love of God without first passing through His fear. All their speech is about God the merciful, the longsuffering and loving. They speak of God Who does not deal with us according to our sins nor punish us according to our iniquities (Psa. 102:10). But, these people do not have a proper understanding of love. They do not practice the fear of God and are indifferent, reckless, and negligent of the commandments. Consequently, they fall.

So, what is love? It is not merely feelings, for the Lord says, "He who has My commandments and keeps them, it is he who loves Me" (John 14:21). While Saint John the Apostle says that perfect love casts out fear, however, in the same epistle he also says: "Let us not love in word or in tongue, but in deed and in truth" (1 John 3:18). What is this active love then? The answer: "For this is the love of God, that we keep His commandments" (1 John 5:3). Surely we keep God's commandments out of our love for Him but this, being a high spiritual level, should be preceded by the keeping of His commandments in His fear.

People are not born saints, but through the fear of God, self-coercion, and self-denial they attain love. Thus says the Apostle Saint Paul, "perfecting holiness in the fear of God" (2 Cor. 7:1). So, how can we perfect holiness in the fear of God? Also, how can we obey the words of Saint Peter the Apostle, "Conduct yourselves throughout the time of your sojourning here in fear" (1 Pet. 1:17)?

A person should start his spiritual life with great caution not to fall into sin. He should evade any pitfalls, temptations, or combats from the devil, esteeming not his own power and resistance but putting before him the words of the Apostle, "Do not be haughty, but fear" (Rom. 11:20). He should fear God, remembering the words of the Lord Jesus Christ: "And do not fear those who kill the body but cannot kill the soul. But rather fear Him

Who is able to destroy both soul and body in hell (Matt.10:28), "...yes, I say to you, fear him!" (Lk. 12:5).

The fear of God's punishment may remain with a person till the last moments of his life. One of the Fathers said, "I fear three moments: the moment my soul leaves my body, the moment I stand before the Judgment seat of our Just God, and the moment when my sentence is carried out on me." Undoubtedly, these three moments are frightening to everyone except those who live in the perfect love of God, those who have reached a state of full communion with Him and are no longer condemned by their conscience. But those who tremble lest any of their actions be exposed on the Day of Judgement, should fear.

It is better for a person to fear while on earth than to fear on the Day of Judgment. On earth, fear leads a person to repent and reconcile with God. But, on Judgment Day fear avails nothing. Fear here gives us a life of reverence, a life of tears, and motivation to return. It is like a fence along the spiritual path guiding us so that we do not deviate from it. So, we pray to God in the Thanksgiving Prayer saying: "Grant us to complete this holy day and all the days of our life in all peace with Your fear."

It is puzzling that some people fear men, but not God. They are afraid to sin before people so as not to be belittled in their eyes, committing sins in secret out of fear of scandal. Those people take advantage of God's love and kindness and misuse their faith in His mercy, tender care, forgiveness, and kind heart which forgave the adulteress and those who denied Him. This sadly leads them to live their spiritual life without sincerity or dedication, as though they can remain in a state
of indifference because God does not reprimand or punish them.

The perfect love that casts out fear belongs to the great saints, not to beginners in repentance nor for those who fall short in their spiritual life. Therefore, live in God's fear and do not jump to the love of God in a theoretical way, claiming that which you do not possess. Do not disdain the fear of God considering it a low level that does not befit you. But be thoroughly confident that if you are faithful in what is little, that is, the fear of God, God will entrust you with much, that is, love. Walk in your spiritual life with discipline and take the proper steps that will lead you to God, without longing for an outward show of spirituality that may mislead you.

It is true that the culmination of spiritual life is perfect love, but you cannot start with the summit. Start with the fear of God, then you will reach the summit without stumbling. This is particularly important for this generation where sin, skepticism, and offenses abound and where unbelievers and blasphemers criticize and mock God's commandments, denying His existence and contending with Him. He who lives in the fear of God advances every day, running to attain his goal. But he who lacks the fear of God digresses every day because he has no fear. He who fears God sees that the path of perfection extending before him and tries with all his might to attain it. Similar to a student who, seeing the difficulty of his course, rushes to study in time to pass his exams; fear prompts him to increase his efforts.

We have before us a long spiritual course which can be summed up in two words: holiness and perfection. The Lord said to us, "Therefore you shall be perfect just as your Father in heaven is perfect" (Matt. 5:48). He commanded us saying: "...be holy" (1 Pet. 1:15). Who of us has reached this level? We ought to fear death overtaking us before attaining our goal, and this fear will prompt us to strive.

❈ Causes of Fearlessness ❈

Why then do we not walk in the fear of God? The following are some of the reasons:

- ✝ One may not fear God because he has not yet examined himself and discovered his real self, true past, sins, and weaknesses. Such a person does not yet realize the spiritual level he should attain, and the necessary effort and struggle required of him.

† Another may not fear God because they have not focused on the Day of Judgment. Reflecting on this day allows us to awake from our slumber. The Church reminds us of this reality every day during the litanies of the Twelfth Hour and during the Midnight Prayer.

† Another person may not fear God because he is dragged by the vortex of the world and does not know where he is going. The world enfolds him in its tumults and drowns him in its waves, overwhelming him with innumerable preoccupations and leaving him no time to think of his destiny or spiritual life. He thus falls into fearlessness as an imitation of the lifestyle of the external world influencing him.

How can he who has not yet reached the fear of God, reach the love of God? How can he reach perfect love which casts out fear? We do not fear because we do not set God before us, we forget Him and His commandments, as the Psalm says about sinners, "... they have not set God before them" (Psa. 53:3). We preoccupy ourselves with this present world and not with the world to come and God's Judgment, resembling the governor Felix's terrified state when Saint Paul the Apostle talked to him about righteousness, self-control, and the Judgement to come (Acts 24:25). We can reach the fear of God if we stay mindful of the Lord's words to the ministers of the churches of Asia, "I know your works" (Rev. 2:2).

❈ Exercises for Fear and Love ❈

These are reasons that hinder the fear of God in us, but there are practices that can help us acquire it.

† Try to fear God at least as much as you fear people.

† Whatever you are afraid to do in the presence of people, do not do before God.

† Whatever thoughts you fear will be known or revealed to people when you wake up from your slumber, do not dwell on before God Who reads and examines all thought.

† Know that all your thoughts, except those for which you repented and were blotted out, will be disclosed before all the creation on the Last Day.

† The hidden sins which you fear committing before people but commit in the dark, try to be ashamed of before God Who sees them.

† Have reverence for God, this will induce you to be ashamed to commit any sin before Him.

† If you fear people and not God Who created those people out of dust, walk before God with prudence and know that He hears and sees all that you do.

† Give reverence to all things related to God and all that is His.

† Stand with reverence and respect during your prayer so that the fear of God may enter your heart. Remember that you stand with respect before your superiors, how can you not behave the same towards God?

† Revere the Holy Bible, for it is the Word of God. Do not put any object on top of it (except the Cross) and handle it with the utmost respect when reading, remembering the words of the deacon at Church: "Stand in the fear of God and listen to the Holy Gospel!" When you give reverence to God's Word, you will fear God Himself.

† Recall the angels of God who surround you, see you, and hear you, and be ashamed.

† Know that your dreadful sins sever you from the communion of angels. Fear their abandonment during the attacks of your malevolent adversaries.

✝   Recall the souls of the saints as well as the souls of your relatives, friends, and even your enemies who have departed, who see you in sin, and have shame.

Walk in the fear of God so that you may reach His love. Remember the words of the Apostle, "Love the brotherhood. Fear God" (1 Peter 2:17), and the words of the angel of the Book of Revelation, "Fear God and give glory to Him" (Rev. 14:7). Remember that the fear of God is mentioned in both the Old and New Testaments.

I have only briefly spoken to you about the fear of God, for it is a large topic which I hope to dwell deeper in in another book, God-willing.

CHAPTER 4

Self-Coercion

Spiritual guides differ in assessing what is the first virtue of the spiritual path. Many believe it is repentance, as it is the turning point of a person's life, it is where he leaves behind the past with all its sins and commences a relationship with God. Others believe it is self-examination, since sitting with oneself precedes repentance. This was the case for Saint Augustine and the Prodigal Son. Some claim that the beginning of the path and the foundation of all virtues is humility and contrition of heart because they lead to repentance and perseverance. While many others believe it to be the knowledge gained through the ministry of the word, for through it, a person discovers valuable principles that influence his thoughts and feelings, leading him to a path of self-accountability, repentance, humility, and contrition of heart. Nevertheless, some saints say that knowledge and self-examination are theoretical, and maybe even external, approaches, whilst the practical way is self-coercion or spiritual struggle.

❈ What is Self-Coercion? ❈

Self-coercion is forcing one's self to walk in the spiritual path. In its true essence, spiritual life is a love of God, goodness, and the Kingdom of Heaven. It is a life of righteousness and purity rooted within the heart and a feeling of joy and desire for a life of communion with God.

Yet, not all people can start at this level. The love of God may be the end point or the summit of one's relationship with God, not the starting point. A person can, however, start with the fear of God, for the Holy Bible says, "The fear of the Lord is the beginning of wisdom" (Prov. 9:10). When a person wakes up from his slumber, the fear of God enters his heart. He begins to fear God's wrath and condemnation for his sins. He worries that death may overtake him at a time when he is not ready, which prompts him to change his path. But how can he change his path? He can change it through self-coercion.

Since the love of God has not yet reigned over his heart, self-coercion is the practical starting point for a spiritual life. A beginner in spirituality is not trained in prayer; he is not used to standing for a long time before God and has no spiritual feelings to inspire him to pray with love, tenderness of heart, reverence, or contemplation. Therefore, self-coercion can help him complete his daily prayers regardless of any temptations of laziness, sleepiness, exhaustion, or fatigue. He can force himself to pray despite the lack of desire to do so, putting before his eyes the words of Saint Isaac the Syrian, "Force yourself to pray in the night, including the psalms with it." This way, a person can force himself to pray; to stand and kneel and to do prostrations. He can force himself to lift up his
hands and concentrate his senses on prayer, controlling his scattered mind and restraining it from wandering.

❊ Self-Coercion and Growth ❊

One of the Fathers once said: "If you wait to reach pure prayer before starting to pray, you will never pray." This is because pure prayer is not the starting point but rather the culmination of the spiritual endeavor. Force yourself to pray, even if your prayer is weighed down by sleep, afflicted by a scattered mind, or void of contemplation. God will look at your exertion, struggle, patient endurance, and perseverance, and will enlighten you with His grace.

This also applies to other virtues. You can force yourself to fast without first having a love for fasting or a desire for hunger. You can exert yourself to read the Holy Bible and contemplate on its words, repent, confess, or attend spiritual meetings. You can even force yourself to forgive others, pay your tithes, and keep the Day of the Lord holy. Self-coercion can also help you restrain the tongue and control the senses, just pray and say: "Set a guard, O Lord, over my mouth; a door of enclosure about my lips" (Psa. 140:3).

❈ Self-Coercion is a Transitional Virtue ❈

Someone may ask: Would God accept a coerced virtue that is void of love? First of all, it is not void of love, for if it were, no one would be able to practice it. Rather, it is a preliminary kind of love that our old self resists due to its attachment to old habits and material things. God accepts our self-coercion as a type of spiritual struggle against the many attacks and hindrances of the devil. He also accepts it as our way to deny ourselves. As Solomon the Wise said, "He who controls his temper is better than he who captures a city" (Prov. 16:30).

God knows that this spiritual endeavor is not easy. He knows that those who begin the spiritual path suffer from the envy of the devils and their assaults. It is likely for the need of forcing one's self to walk in the spiritual path that the Lord said, "Enter by the narrow gate; for wide is the gate and broad is the way that leads to destruction, and there are many who go in by it. Because narrow is the gate and difficult is the way which leads to life, and there are few who find it" (Matt. 7:13,14). Yet, the gate does not remain narrow the entire way, but
only at the beginning. The more a person practices a spiritual act, the more he finds pleasure in it and the more it attracts him, pushing him to pursue it with an ardent heart. In this manner, one may start to pray by forcing himself. Once he finds the spiritual enjoyment of prayer, he will begin to practice it with diligence
and love.

The devil, however, ridicules this self-coercion and seeks to twist it as a means to halt our spiritual endeavors. He asks you, "Is it decent to speak to God by forcing yourself to pray? Where is the love of which David the Prophet said, 'I will lift up my hands in Your Name. My soul shall be satisfied as with marrow and fatness' (Psa. 62:5, 6)?" Then, he calls for you to stop your prayer for the sake of a notion of pure prayer that is full of love and awe! It is impossible for you to start with such perfection. Yet, it is crucial for the devil to stop you from praying or attempting any spiritual act by mocking your state of self-coercion.

However, God looks upon the inarticulate cries of a little infant as the beginning of talking, and to the toddling of a baby as the primary steps of walking. The world's champions in jumping, running, and swimming began their childhood with awkward movements, then progressively reached perfection. That is why we do not disdain self-coercion, nor does God despise it. Rather, He encourages it so that a person can grow and walk towards Divine love. It is important, however, to remember that self-coercion is only a step that should take you from forced practices to revered habits.

An example of a self-coerced step that leads to love is almsgiving. The Holy Bible says that "God loves a cheerful giver" (2 Cor. 9:7). Will you refrain from giving until you reach the standard of a cheerful giver? or the standard of "he who gives with liberality" (Rom. 12:8)? Why should the poor or those in need of your donation bear the brunt of your not having reached this standard? The right attitude is for you to give even if, initially, by force. Force yourself to pay the tithes for the sake of the poor who need it, then force yourself to give God your first fruits, vows, and all that is due to Him of your possessions. Soon, you will begin to disburse all that you have for others without any force.

You may ask, "How?" The more you perceive people's happiness and relief from what you give, the happier you become, and you will become a more cheerful and generous giver. Self-coercion will eventually come to an end because it is a transitional, not a constant, virtue.

God rewards virtues completed with love as well as coercion, for

He takes into account the labor necessary to abandon sins willingly and overcome obstacles, both externally and internally.

Self-coercion tames your self and your will. An animal initially resists the laying of a yoke on its neck and may attempt to flee. But when tamed, it starts to easily bend its neck under the yoke and carry out its duties quietly and willingly. Resistance was only the primary stage; its grumbling and defiance were replaced with contentment. How much more deserving is he who willingly obeys to coerce himself, believing it to be a transitional stage?

Spiritual exercises often start with self-coercion. A spiritually mature person naturally does good, but a beginner needs exercises. He may fail at the beginning, but through persistence and spiritual struggle he can transform his coerced practices into lasting, established characteristics. Saint Paul the Apostle says, "Everywhere and in all things, I have learned both to be full and to be hungry, both to abound and to suffer need" (Phil. 4:12). The more difficult the practice is, the greater the reward. Self-coercion strengthens one's will and directs it towards goodness.

❈ Benefits of Self-Coercion ❈

Self-coercion is highly effective at overcoming the bad habits that have long dwelt inside a person, subduing, humiliating, and enslaving him. It is a rebellion against the will and a war on the ego, for he who surrenders to his desires, comfort, and convenience loses his self.

Coercion brings the self under submission, subduing it to one's orders and forcing it to walk the path that leads to the love of God. We often use coercion in raising our children. If we leave them to their own will and desires, it will result in their perdition. When love, kindness, convincing, and nagging fail, coercion may be necessary for their own good.

Jonah the Prophet could not force himself to obey God, so God forced him. When he escaped from God, God ordered a great fish to swallow him and bring him back to obedience. Those who do not return to God by love, return to Him by force through various trials and afflictions. It is thus better for a person to force himself than be forced by events and trials.

One difference between saints and ordinary people is that saints coerce themselves to practice virtues until they become habits and passions. They have bodies like ours that suffer from hunger and thirst, but they force them to fast. They become weary and exhausted, yet still force themselves to vigils, like Saint Bishoy who used to tie his hair with a rope to the ceiling of his cell to resist sleeping during his night prayers. Likewise, David the Prophet made a covenant saying, "Surely I will not enter my dwelling, or go up to the comfort of my bed; I will not give sleep to my eyes or slumber to my eyelids, until I find a place for the Lord" (Ps. 131:3-5).

❋ Advice and Spiritual Exercises ❋

✝ Do not surrender to the love of comfort nor to the call of lusts.

✝ Do not spoil yourself, rather have faith that self-coercion will end once you find pleasure and love in the life of virtue.

✝ Put before you an important spiritual principle: the biggest war we fight in our spiritual life is the war against ourselves. If we prevail internally through self-coercion, we will overcome every other external war.

✝ Do not carry out every thought that enters your mind, nor any desire that knocks on the door of your heart. If you cannot refrain, postpone the matter for a while, then force yourself to keep postponing. During this period of postponement, the grace of God may visit you and grant you rest.

† Know that self-coercion comes under the Lord's commandment to carry the Cross (Matt. 16:24), because "those who are Christ's have crucified the flesh with its passions and desires" (Gal. 5:24).

† Try to resist your ego and desires.

† Lay down for yourself a fixed spiritual discipline and force yourself to put it into practice.

† Do not permit yourself some exceptions, for that can lead to slackness, indifference, and lack of seriousness in your spiritual endeavor.

The principle of self-coercion appears in the words of the Lord, "And if your right eye causes you to sin, pluck it out and cast it from you...And if your right hand causes you to sin, cut it off and cast it from you" (Matt. 5:29,30). Thus, do not yield to your eyes when they desire to look, but restrict them, restrain your hands also. Restrain your tongue from talking, for Saint James the Apostle says: bridle, tame, and control the tongue.

Just like the nations lay down laws and punishments, God also gives us commandments and penalties. A person should force himself to abandon sins and do good before he is forced to do so by any laws, commandments, or punishments. It is necessary for goodness to spring from a person's heart, through his own will, without compulsion or promise of reward.

Let your conscience force you and not the law. Force yourself to do good before you force others. And if you err, rebuke your inner self instead of receiving an external punishment.

CHAPTER 5

Spiritual Conduct

The spiritual person walks according to the Spirit. He walks as the Spirit directs and leads him, and not according to the flesh and its desires. Whoever walks according to the Spirit is acceptable to God, while whoever walks according to the flesh falls under condemnation. This is why Saint Paul the Apostle said, "There is therefore now no condemnation to those who are in Christ Jesus, who do not walk according to the flesh, but according to the Spirit" (Rom. 8:1).

Naturally, the spiritual person cares for his spirit—for its nourishment, health, and growth. In order to keep it strong and flourishing, he provides it with the necessary nourishment: prayer, fasting, spiritual readings, contemplations, prostrations, spiritual gatherings, spiritual retreats, and spiritual guidance. His spirit flourishes as he lives a life of virtue, loving God and living in repentance to preserve his purity.

Notwithstanding, the vast majority of people are more concerned with their bodies than their spirits. They give all their attention to the flesh and its needs—from food and drink to clothing, housing, entertainment, and adornment. Their thoughts and emotions are obsessed with satisfying the body's lusts and pleasures, even if it conflicts with the purity of their spirit.

These people neglect the words of the Apostle, "For to be carnally minded is death, but to be spiritually minded is life and peace. Because the carnal mind is enmity against God…So then, those who are in the flesh cannot please God" (Rom. 8:6-8). Carnal people cannot inherit the Kingdom of God because it is a spiritual kingdom where only those who walk according to the Spirit abide.

When the Apostle talked about the love of the world as enmity with God, he said: "For all that is in the world - the lust of the flesh, the lust of the eyes, and the pride of life" (1 John 2:16), placing the lust of the flesh as first in worldly matters.

❈ Is the Body Sinful? ❈

Here we ask a pressing question: Is the body sinful?

No, the body is neither sinful nor evil, otherwise God would not have created it. It suffices that God Himself took a body. Moreover, if the body was sinful, we would not venerate the relics of the saints. The Apostle tells us, "Or do you not know that your body is the temple of the Holy Spirit who is in you?" and "Do you not know that your bodies are members of Christ?" (1 Cor. 6:19,15). Therefore, the human body is not evil at all.

God promised to raise this body on the Last Day as a spiritual body of light (1 Cor. 15).

Our bodies are holy because they were immersed in the water of baptism, consecrated, and took on a new nature. They were anointed with the Holy Chrism of Myron and became a temple for the Lord (1 Cor. 3:16). We respect the body and look upon it with dignity, whether our own or that of other people, remembering the words of the Apostle, "If anyone defiles the temple of God, God will destroy him" (1 Cor. 3:17). Therefore, glorify God in your body and in your spirit, which are God's" (1 Cor. 6:20).

We can glorify God in and with our body. Does the body not join the spirit in worshipping God? The spirit prays and the body stands, kneels, prostrates, and lifts pure hands and eyes towards God. The body fasts and toils in service and in helping others. If we respect the body accordingly, we will never humiliate or defile it.

The body is also like a church: it is holy, consecrated with Myroon, and is the dwelling place of the Spirit of God. This small church should offer praises, prayers, hymns, psalmody, and spiritual songs (Eph. 5:19). These are all lifted up to God as incense, just like the words of the Psalm: "Let my prayer be set before You as incense, the lifting up of my hands as the evening sacrifice" (Psa. 140:2).

This is the sound spiritual view of the body. It is not sinful if we use and understand it in a spiritual way. It is something holy, like the bodies of Adam and Eve before sin, the righteous during Resurrection, and the living when they bless God. How, then, can we keep the body holy?

❖ Submission of the Body to the Spirit ❖

The body is holy when it submits to the spirit; and not vice versa. When the spirit guides the body, the person walks in a spiritual manner, conforming to the words of the Apostle, "I beseech you therefore, brethren, by the mercies of God, that you present your bodies a living sacrifice, holy, acceptable to God, which is your reasonable service. And do not be conformed to this world" (Rom. 12:1-2). Thus, the body becomes a holy and living sacrifice.

On the other hand, when the body resists and does not submit to the spirit, the Holy Bible says, "For the flesh lusts against the Spirit, and the Spirit against the flesh; and these are contrary to one another" (Gal. 5:17). The Apostle Saint Paul does not say this about all bodies, rather about the sinful bodies that resist the work of the Spirit and lust against it, creating an inner conflict between one's body and spirit. The saints were not like this. Their bodies were united with their spirits in their spiritual work. That is why God rewards the body and grants it to rejoice with the spirit in the eternal bliss of His Kingdom.

Saint Paul the Apostle said: "But I discipline my body and bring it into subjection, lest, when I have preached to others, I myself should become disqualified" (1 Cor. 9:27). The Desert Fathers practiced this until their bodies became completely submissive to their spirits. They did not grant their body lustful desires, but made it unite with their spirit in spiritual practices such as fasting, vigil, and prostrations.

The body itself is not a sin, but the lust of the flesh is. Our forefathers Adam and Eve fell into the lust of the flesh when they looked at the Tree of Knowledge of Good and Evil and saw that it was good for food, pleasant to the eyes, and a tree desirable to make one wise (Gen. 3:6). This initiated a deviation towards desiring what is material and carnal. But the Holy Bible warns, "For if you live according to the flesh you will die; but if by the Spirit you put to death the deeds of the body, you will live" (Rom. 8:13).

Saints embarked on deeds of mortification, putting to death the passions of the body. Likewise, we entreat the Lord Jesus during the Prayer of the Ninth Hour saying: "Mortify our carnal senses." Our carnal senses die when they no longer insinuate the passions and desires of the heart. At this point, the spiritual senses live and move by the love of God.

The Holy Bible says, "But you are not in the flesh but in the Spirit, if indeed the Spirit of God dwells in you" (Rom. 8:9). If a person submits the body and lives by the Spirit, he will enjoy a life of victory over the world. His body and spirit will be in harmony and will have the same desires, cooperating in every righteous deed.

❈ The Body and Sin ❈

The body that sins is one that rebels against the spirit or subjects it to its lusts. It defiles the spirit, which makes it lose its Divine image and fall into condemnation on the Day of Judgment. A sinning body defiles one of God's temples. Since the body is a temple of God, he who sins against it is like he who destroys a holy church in which God dwells.

A sinning body not only rebels against its own spirit, but also against the Spirit of God Who dwells in it. If we consider the person whose spirit prevails and leads the body to a life of holiness like an angel of God in heaven, it follows that a person whose body controls and directs the spirit is like an animal.

A body that lives in its lusts is considered dead, even if it is throbbing with life. As the Apostle said, "The body is dead because of sin" (Rom. 8:10). That is why the Lord said to the Angel of the Church of Sardis, "I know your works, that you have a name that you are alive, but you are dead" (Rev. 3:1). And about the indulgent widow, Saint Paul said: "she who lives in pleasure is dead while she is alive" (1 Tim. 5:6).

True life is in God, and he who is separated from God by sin is considered dead even if he is alive. As the father described his prodigal son by saying: "for this my son was dead" (Lk. 15:24). He who repents returns to life once more. Thus, when the Prodigal Son repented, his father declared that his son "was dead and now is alive again" (Lk. 15:24). That is why a person who cares for his spirit, cares for his eternity.

❈ Caring for the Spirit ❈

The Apostle says, "To be spiritually minded is life and peace" (Rom. 8:6). A person should always put before him that he has one spirit, if he directs it to the way of salvation, he profits everything, but if he loses this spirit, he loses everything. As the Lord Jesus Christ said, "For what is a man profited if he gains the whole world and loses his own soul" (Matt. 16:26).

He who walks in the spiritual path concerns himself wholeheartedly with purifying his spirit and connecting it with God, aspiring that it inherits the Kingdom of God in the blissful eternity. He walks and grows in the Spirit, becoming a spiritual person. He is restored to the Image of God and preserves himself in God. For the spirit is the breath which God breathed in man, making him a living spirit, whereas the body is the earthly element that was created out of dust.

Through spiritual conduct, man becomes like the angels. He forms a friendship and a connection with God, His angels, and the whole spiritual world. In fact, he himself becomes an angel of God. His behavior, words, and relations become spiritual as the

Spirit governs his whole life.

Therefore, my brother, consider how you walk. Do you walk in the Spirit or in the flesh? The Holy Bible urges us, "Walk in the Spirit, and you shall not fulfill the lust of the flesh" (Gal. 5: 16), "be filled with the Spirit" (Eph. 5:18). For a person who grows spiritually not only walks in the Spirit but is also filled with it.

❈ Your Spirit and the Spirit of God ❈

The spiritual person submits his body to his spirit and submits his spirit to the Spirit of God. This becomes proof of his sonship to God. To this effect the Holy Bible says, "For as many as are led by the Spirit of God, these are sons of God" (Rom. 8:14). If the Spirit of God directs a person, he does not sin and "the wicked one does not touch him" (1 John 3:9), (1 John 5:18). Indeed, this is how the children of God are made known.

The spiritual life is not only limited to the negative aspect of abandoning sin, but also the positive aspect of the manifestation of the fruit of the Spirit. Concerning this the Apostle said, "But the fruit of the Spirit is love, joy, peace, longsuffering, kindness, goodness, faithfulness, gentleness, self-control" (Gal. 5:22,23). Describing those who walk in the Spirit, he said: "those who are Christ's have crucified the flesh with its passions and desires" (Gal. 5:24) and added, "If we live in the Spirit, let us also walk in the Spirit" (Gal. 5:25). How can we say that we are children of God if we are not led by the Spirit of God? How can we say that we live in the Spirit if the fruit of the Spirit is not apparent in our life?

A person who is led by the Spirit of God does not quench, grieve, or resist Him, but submits to His work within him. He is a malleable instrument with which God carries out His holy will. He does not betray God by opening the doors of his heart or mind to anything contrary to Him. Rather, he cooperates with the Spirit of God and enters into a fellowship with the Holy Spirit (2 Cor. 13:14), becoming a partaker of the Divine Nature (2 Peter 1:4) and working for his salvation and the salvation of those around him.

Thus, spiritual life is the conduct of your spirit and the spirit of God. It is where your spirit becomes adorned with virtues, ready to meet God "as a bride adorned for her husband" (Rev. 21:2). There, your spirit is adorned with love and humility, faith and labor, adorned with the "ornament of a gentle and quiet Spirit, which is very precious in the sight of God" (1 Peter 3:4), as Saint Peter the Apostle said.

Therefore, concern yourself with the beauty of your spirit so that when you take off your earthly body, your spirit will be acceptable in heaven. For if you have the fragrant aroma of Christ, even the devils will revere your spirit: "A thousand may fall at your side, and ten thousand at your right hand; but it shall not come near you" (Psa. 90:7). Preserve, then, the indwelling of His Spirit within you.

Do you want to test yourself and see whether or not you walk in the Spirit? Consider this question: Do you fear the devils, or do they fear you because the Spirit of God dwells in you?

Walk, my brother, in the Spirit and you will reach this level. In every deed, trust that God works with you through His Holy Spirit.

CHAPTER 6

Uprightness

❧ The Meaning of Uprightness ❧

A spiritual person is an upright person. He is upright in his thoughts, conscience, and conduct before both God and men. What is the meaning of this uprightness and what are its features? How can it be attained? How can we test it and distinguish it?

An upright person is a just person. He does not behave unjustly, whether consciously or unconsciously. He does not mix truthfulness with falsehood. He walks a straight path and does not stray, as the Divine Inspiration says, "Do not turn to the right or to the left" (Prov. 4:27), that is, do not go to extremes.

❧ Uprightness is Against Extremism ❧

Exaggeration in the spiritual path is not acceptable, whether in words or behavior. Exaggeration is a type of lying, for it does not give an accurate representation of reality. Exaggerated behavior can be a shade of extremism like the Pharisees. Saint Paul refers to his life before faith saying, "according to the strictest sect of our religion I lived a Pharisee" (Acts 26:5).

Those who are strict with themselves become accustomed to rigidity and often deal with others in a like manner. Their judgment becomes overbearing, harsh, and distorted. The Lord Jesus Christ rebuked the Scribes and the Pharisees because they bound heavy burdens that were hard to bear and laid them on men's shoulders (Matt. 23:4). The Pharisees' extreme views made them cruel and judgmental. As a result, they made people view the Kingdom of God as unattainable, causing them to fall into despair. They closed the Kingdom of heaven before people; they neither got in themselves nor allowed those who were entering to go in (Matt. 23:13).

Extremism is not sustainable. For example, a person may be extreme in the way he fasts for a period of time. He may think he has reached a high spiritual level when suddenly, he is unable to continue. In fact, that person may revert back to a much lower level than those who advance in the spiritual life slowly and in progressive steps. This also applies to prostrations and other ascetic practices. To forsake the sins of the tongue, many become extreme, imposing on themselves severe silence exercises that cannot be sustained for a long period of time. This can cause them to fall into other sins that ruin their relationships with people and distance them from uprightness.

Moreover, unstable behavior that fluctuates to extremes is not upright and does not follow the way of the fathers. Spiritual fathers counsel their disciples to avoid extremity for two reasons: (1) extremity does not agree with the truth and (2) secondly, it lacks stability moves a person from one extreme to the other. Fluctuation does not comply with the uprightness that belongs to the sound spiritual life. For this reason, the Fathers recommend gradualness. That is, by starting simply and easily, without self-conceit and haughtiness. Then, to gradually progress towards your goal until you attain it. They used to say: "Little with continuity is better than much with intermittence."

When anyone is able to sustain a spiritual endeavor for a long period of time, it settles in his heart and abounds in a quiet, progressive, and steadfast manner. This is much better than spiritual leaps which do not last and are often followed by spiritual relapses. Such leaps are perilous and, in most cases, are reaped by the devil of vainglory.

Uprightness is not only the opposite of extremism, but of falsehood as well.

❈ Uprightness is Against Falsehood ❈

If it is wrong to be extreme even in what one believes is right, what then shall we say about being extreme in what is false? A person might walk in falsehood out of ignorance, yet he is still condemned as behaving immorally. His way is not upright, for it is against truth and righteousness, whether or not he is aware of it. Deep are the words of the Holy Bible: "There is a way that seems right to man, but its end is the way of death" (Prov. 16:25; 14; 12). Falsehood is one such way; its end is death, regardless of the way it seems to man.

Pride may lead a person to perceive his behavior as upright, whereas it may be the complete opposite of reality. In this respect, the Holy Bible says, "The way of a fool is right in his own eyes" (Prov. 12:15). Uprightness requires a humble heart that is capable of perceiving its errors and correcting its ways. He who is prideful retains his false behavior because he refuses to acknowledge his mistakes. Here, we observe the close relationship between uprightness and humility. A haughty person does not thoroughly know the reality of who he is, he does not recognize his weaknesses nor acknowledge them. Hence, he is a fool.

A person may also walk in falsehood out of illness. For example, a person suffering from a mental illness may think certain individuals are persecuting him, so he starts to hate, resist, revile, and criticize them, further complicating his mental state. He may experience a constant sense of danger around him when none exists.

Such a person is not upright in his behavior as a result of his mental illness, he is not held accountable for his actions for they are beyond his control, yet those actions are not upright. Falsehood is falsehood, regardless of accountability, for it is not the mentally ill individual who is not upright, but rather his actions. Truthfulness cannot be mixed with falsehood, for falling into falsehood distorts the uprightness of your ways and does not comply with the characteristics of the spiritual path. Nevertheless, if you confess your sins and straighten your ways, you are considered repentant.

Perilous is the person who considers the falsehood in which he walks a type of uprightness. He clothes it with robes of virtue and considers himself truthful, despite all his errors. Consequently he lives without repentance and lacks uprightness in both his conscience and intellect.

How dangerous is that immoral conscience? It commits sins yet remains untroubled, for it has become desensitized. That conscience has lost its discernment, its values, its moral sense of judgment, and thus lacks integrity. However, if such a person were to accept spiritual instruction, there would be hope to regain the spiritual discernment and uprightness of the mind, conscience, and behavior.

❈ Uprightness is Against Hypocrisy ❈

Some people try to cover up their falsehood through hypocrisy, outwardly appearing as upright while internally, they are the opposite. Even though they may appear to people as righteous, they are sinners. They are like whitewashed tombs which appear beautiful from
the outside, but inside are full of dead men's bones and all uncleanness.

Their hypocrisy consists of two transgressions: the lack of inward uprightness, and the outward pretense and the outward pretence of uprightness, which is also a dishonest act. Thus, they fall into two sins simultaneously. If a person who does good deeds stemming from a desire to appear righteous before others is considered a hypocrite, how much so is one who does no good deeds but appears upright and virtuous to people? This is double the hypocrisy!

Judas was of such kind. He appeared to be greeting Christ with a kiss, yet he was surrendering Him to His enemies. He sat next to Him, ate with Him, and dipped his morsel in the same dish even though he had conspired against Him and received the price. Judas's betrayal aside, his continuity in following Christ as a disciple, eating with Him, and kissing Him was another type of transgression, one manifested in hypocrisy and a pretense of love.

Delilah, in her dealing with Samson, displayed this same blend of betrayal and hypocrisy. She showed him love and intimacy while handing him over to his enemies. The devil also deals with us with the same hypocrisy, manipulating it to a higher degree. He pretended to offer Adam and Eve the path to glory yet was working toward their destruction.

A hypocrite has two faces, two tongues, and many tricks. An example of this is Balaam who tried to take the money of Balak the son of Zippor and construct seven altars for the Lord (Num. 22,23). He said, "How shall I curse whom God has not cursed? Must I not take heed to speak what the Lord has put in my mouth?" (Num. 23:8,12). But at the same time, he presented Balak with the advice that would destroy the people (Rev. 2:14). Balaam thought he was justified because his tongue did not curse the people, but his heart was seeking their destruction.

An upright person's heart and tongue always follow the same pure path. The Lord Jesus Christ criticized those whose tongues and hearts follow different paths, repeating the phrase of the Old Testament: "These people draw near to Me with their mouth, and honor Me with their lips, but their heart is far from Me" (Matt. 15:8; Isa. 29:13). When an upright person utters a word of love or praise with his lips, his heart bears the same feeling. There is no contradiction between the heart and the tongue; for, contradiction indicates a lack of uprightness. In this contradiction falls those who use flattering words, untrue praise, and insincerity. Among those were the false prophets who said to King Ahab that he would prevail (1 Kings 22:13-22).

Politics and hidden intentions do not lead an upright person, nor do they alter his conscience or tongue. An upright person does not use hypocrisy for the sake of achieving something or gaining fame. He is the same inwardly and outwardly, as one person. He does not behave contrary to his conscience in order to please people, nor does he speak anything inconsistent with what he believes in his heart to be true.

❋ Uprightness is Against Deception ❋

Hypocrisy contradicts uprightness because it attempts to combine two opposing paths, by means of deception.

Jacob was not upright when he deceived his father, Isaac, and told him that he was his firstborn son Esau (Gen. 27:19). Nor was he upright when he put the skins of the kids of the goats on his hands and on the smooth part of his neck.

His mother, Rebekah, was not upright when she advised him to do all this, promising him that his curse will be on her (Gen. 27:13).

Joseph's brothers were not upright when they deceived their father Jacob by dipping Joseph's colorful tunic into the blood of a kid of a goat so that their father might think that he was devoured by a wild beast (Gen. 37:31-33).

An upright person is honest and clear with his words, he does not lie, deceive, or seek to achieve his purpose or solve his problems through deceit. He believes that deception is not upright and would despise himself if it ever led him to his purpose.

For deceit is against truth, and he who is upright is truthful and does not tolerate unfairness. He reaches his goals using upright methods, believing that the means are as important as the aim.

❋ Uprightness is Against Craftiness ❋

An upright person also rejects craftiness. When a crooked person does not reach his aim through upright means, he employs trickery. If he fails, he employs craftiness, going around in circles.

But an upright person rejects all crooked and devious ways that conceal one's intentions and make him reach his aim deceptively.

Those who utilize this approach present secondary, less important reasons, in hopes that the second, third, or fourth reason may be of more interest to the listener, even if it has no connection to the main subject. They may provide such reasons to obtain the listener's approval in one way or another, while concealing the primary reason. Although those secondary reasons may be true, they are not entirely truthful, but are used as an artifice to deceive the listener.

Similarly, utilizing exaggeration, whether in evaluating matters or in describing their benefits and disadvantages, to convince the listener does not align with uprightness, nor does it conform with the speaker's respect of his own conscience or that of others.

❈ Uprightness and Trust ❈

An upright person earns the trust of all who communicate or converse with him, his uprightness gives a glimpse of his spirituality and religious devotion. Uprightness is not just a social trait, but it is one of the characteristics of the spiritual path. We say this because some may be involved in service within the church but employ false, worldly means to fulfill their service. This can cause others to stumble.

A spiritual person needs to constantly accustom himself to uprightness, regardless of the cost or effort he expends for its sake. For even if he thinks he will suffer a loss from being upright, it will be a material loss yet a spiritual gain. Any profit or benefit that may come through crooked means has to be rejected, knowing that it is not from God.

A person's eternal life, adoption, and membership in His body are worth more than any worldly benefit and must be blameless before all. Thus, we should always put the example of the saintly Fathers before our eyes and try to follow in their steps.

CHAPTER 7

Spiritual Goals

Values are the important, valuable elements that guide a person in his life. He who wishes to live a life of virtue clings to his values and considers them as principles before commencing any endeavor. What are the things you deem valuable, and which of them guide your life?

People hold different values. While a spiritual person may have high values constantly set before him, others live in the world without values at all, or have values that are not spiritual upon which they construct their lives. Whatever the case, inside every person's heart, there is one thing he believes is of utmost value and to which he directs all his efforts and emotions. Some concentrate all their effort on wealth, others on fame and grandeur, while others on success and high positions. Where each person concentrates his efforts determines how important he deems his values.

Here, we come across an important subject, namely, the goal and the means.

❊ The Goal and the Means ❊

A person may put before him a certain goal, valuing it above all else and sparing no thought to the means he will employ to reach it, whether it be lies, deception, falsehood, or cunning. If he fulfils it, he relishes his success, even if that success came at a great cost for others. He who can step over others to reach his goal no doubt is a self-seeker, living without values, and misjudging both the aim and the means.

On the other hand, a spiritual person should set before him a good aim and utilize good means to achieve it. Such are the people who have values and principles.

We may now ask, what does success mean?

❦ The Meaning of Success ❦

Every person yearns to succeed. Success is often a goal people place before themselves. But what does success mean? Every person rejoices over the success of achieving a goal, however improper that aim may be. But this is not the meaning of success we are referring to.

We are talking here about the true meaning of success, for even evil doers rejoice when they succeed in their evil deeds.

Success is victory over one's self, not over others. Success is attaining purity of heart, not merely accomplishing your goals. Success is having the Kingdom of God in your heart and making every other goal be within that primary goal of the Kingdom. If your success is outside these values, then it is a failure and not a success. Many rejoice on earth while heaven laments their state, for while they think they have succeeded in the present world, they forfeit eternal life.

This leads us to an important value: caring for your salvation and eternity.

❦ Caring for Your Salvation ❦

A spiritual person's foremost priority is his salvation; it occupies the whole of his concern and thoughts. His salvation is the most valuable part of his life. Every deed or goal that conflicts with his eternal life is absolutely and unquestionably rejected. Such a person considers his present life as preparation for eternal life. His concern for his eternal salvation gives his present life a pure, spiritual direction and keeps him steadfast in God, his love for Him, and observing His commandments.

On the other hand, those who have made worldly positions and pleasures their highest priority do not share this spiritual attitude. They are preoccupied by worldly matters that overwhelm their thoughts and cause them to neglect their eternal life. For this reason, the Lord Jesus Christ presented us with a spiritual principle to set before our eyes, "For what is a man profited if he gains the whole world, and loses his own soul? Or what will a man give in exchange for his soul?" (Matt. 16:26).

Dear reader, ask yourself what value your salvation has in your life. Is it one of the primary values which you uphold and are always mindful of? Or is it not of your concern at all, since you are preoccupied with various other concerns and have forgotten the Lord's words to Martha, "you are worried and troubled about many things. But one thing is needed" (Lk. 10:41,42)? What are those other concerns of this present world which call for more consideration than your eternity? Has the time not come for you to fix your spiritual balance and reassess your concerns so that eternity may take its due consideration in your heart, mind, and time?

When we speak of eternity, we speak of your eternity and that of other people as well. We speak of the extent to which you value the Kingdom of God within you and for all people, the extent of your vigilance to enter this Kingdom together with everyone you know. Here, it becomes apparent that holy zeal and service constitute important characteristics of the spiritual path and are values that should lead your life.

The more you value eternal life, the less valuable the world becomes in your eyes. Therefore, one of the characteristics of the spiritual life is to deem nothing valuable in this present world, keeping in mind the Apostle's words, "Do not love the world or the things in the world. If anyone loves the world, the love of the Father is not in him" (1 John 2:15).

Ask yourself with honesty: Do you value this world? Is it the place where your life, enjoyment, and desire lie? Is it so attractive to you that you cannot do without its pleasures and entertainment, and would grieve if you departed it? Or are the world and all things in it mere rubbish to you as Saint Paul said (Phil. 3:8)?

Solomon the Wise experienced both of these conditions. When he saw the world as a place of pleasure, he said, "Whatever my eyes desired I did not keep from them" (Ecc. 2:10), and when it lost its value in his sight, he declared that "all was vanity and grasping for the wind. There was no profit under the sun" (Ecc. 2:11).

The way you interact with the world depends on how valuable you see it. Do you see the world as trivial, vain, and grasping for the wind? Or is it a passion strongly pulling you towards it: the lust of the flesh, the lust of the eyes, and the pride of life (1 John 2:16)? May your evaluation of the world result in you believing in its vanity and that it is passing away together with the lust of it (1 John 2:17).

Valuing eternal life gave rise to asceticism, monasticism and celibacy. Even martyrdom was a fruit of the belief in the value of eternal life and in the vanity of this world. Saint Augustine also experienced the various desires of the world, but when it lost its value in his sight, he declared, "I found myself on top of the world when I felt within myself that I neither desire nor fear anything."[1]

Therefore, to lead a person to the love of God, he must first amend his view of the world, his values, and his outlook on matters. The Apostle confirms this saying, "Be transformed by the renewing of your mind" (Rom. 12:2). What is the renewing of the mind but a change of mindset and a correction of values so that its outlook on matters be straightened and acquire a spiritual attitude?

Here we ask: What is your evaluation of your spiritual and bodily needs?

---

[1] While it is unclear which passage HH refers to here, please see Confessions, Book VI. See also Words of Spiritual Benefit, Ch. 35 on "Fear."

❊ The Spirit and the Body ❊

There is no doubt that the majority of people give all or most of their attention to their body, in terms of its nourishment, health, strength, and beauty. They constantly provide it with what it needs in terms of food, medicine, treatment, rest, activity, and relaxation. In like manner, they care for the health of the bodies of their children and relatives.

Yet, they do not give the same attention to their spirit; and its needs are often neglected. That is why peoples' spirits weaken, having received neither adequate spiritual nourishment nor care through spiritual exercises such as reading, contemplation, praise, spiritual gatherings, prayer, and ascetic practices.

Thus, the extent to which we value our spirit determines how we lead our life. Valuing the spirit more than the body motivates us to care for the spiritual values and means necessary to promote our spiritual growth and advance along the spiritual path. Let us give an example of a spiritual value, prayer.

❊ Prayer ❊

How do you perceive prayer? Is it a means of help during times of affliction to which you turn when you need God? Is it an obligation, such that if you do not keep it, your conscience reprimands you about your negligence? Or is it spiritual nourishment, without which your spiritual life grows lukewarm? Is it an enjoyment, the sweetness of which you yearn for? Do you forget the whole world when you pray, wishing to prolong the time of your conversation with God?

Your evaluation of prayer affects your spirituality during it as well as your consistency. Examine yourself regarding prayer and give it its proper attention. The saints tell us that prayer is like breathing; indispensable and accompanying you at all times and in all places.

We sometimes err by valuing our abilities more than prayer. We depend on our perseverance, intelligence, and experiences instead.

Prayer becomes our last priority —we pray if we have time, if we remember, or if others remind us. This is because we do not give prayer its proper due, and the same applies to all other spiritual practices.

Thus, reevaluate your life. Realize the importance of God and the importance of your life with Him. Then, you will be able to manage your life in a more proper manner. If you need to reassess your life with God, then you, undoubtedly, need to do the same regarding your relationship with others.

❈ Your Relationship with Others ❈

What is the value of people in your eyes? Do you consider every person your brother or sister? Do you love them and concern yourself with them? Do you care for everyone as God does, of course, within your ability? Are you mindful of people's feelings? All people? Do you value the soul? Is the soul of every person precious in your sight? Do you love every person as you love yourself, caring for him and his interests as you would for the dearest of your friends, so that whatever befalls him befalls you, whatever gladdens him gladdens you, and whatever injures him injures you?

Valuing the human soul and caring for the rights and feelings of others is a characteristic of the spiritual person. My brother, the more you value the human soul, the more you respect all people, not daring to hurt anyone's feelings, or to sin against or with any person, nor cause anyone to stumble. You will fear that God may request their blood from you on the Last Day.

You may care for the feelings of the elders, yet, you may neglect and ignore the little ones. But God is the God of all: He cares for the superior as He cares for the assistant. He cares for the elderly as well as the young, the educated and the uneducated. He shines His sun on the just and the unjust and sends His rain on the righteous and the wicked. No one is forgotten by God. Every soul is dear to Him, He looks after each one as the Good Shepherd Who gives His life for His sheep (John 10).

Taking God as your model, you should treat others in a similar manner. If the human soul has this great value in your sight, you will respect the freedom and rights of others. You will not provoke anyone, treat anyone unjustly, hurt or slander anyone. Rather, you will embrace everyone with your love.

The value of the human soul calls you to serve and to sacrifice yourself for the sake of the salvation of others. He who believes in the value of every soul will say with Saint Paul, "Who is weak, and I am not weak? Who is made to stumble, and I do not burn with indignation?" (2 Cor. 11:29). Always remember how the Lord went to look for one soul. No single soul went unnoticed among the flock. Neither did it lose any of its importance in the presence of the ninety-nine (Lk. 15:4-7). God toils for the sake of every single soul.

❊ Rest and Toil ❊

An ordinary person is concerned with his own comfort, even if it comes at the expense of others. But a person with values finds true rest when he toils for the sake of making others comfortable. To him, the meaning of rest is providing comfort to other people, not to himself. He believes rest is that of his conscience, not of his body.

That person is fully aware that true comfort is found in eternal life, rather than on earth. In eternity, everyone will receive his reward according to his labor (1 Cor. 3:8), which is why toiling for the sake of goodness is what the spiritual man concerns himself with.

CHAPTER 8

Commitment

Commitment is one of the most important characteristics of the spiritual path. He who does not adhere to his commitments is by no means spiritual. A spiritual person commits himself to every word he says, every promise he makes, and every covenant between him and God. He abides by certain principles, values, morals, and spiritual rules. He lives responsibly and is respected by all.

Every word he says has great weight and importance and is better than any written agreement. Even if he does not speak and merely nods his head as a sign of approval, it is acknowledged that he will adhere to his agreement without the need for any witnesses or signatures. His commitment is proof of his reliability and of his respect to his word and promises, a proof of honorable conduct. He is committed to what he decrees and to what he imposes on himself.

He is also committed to his spiritual principles and relationship with God, obeying Him and keeping His commandments. The Holy Bible gives us wonderful examples of the virtue of commitment:

Abraham the Patriarch held fast to the life of obedience and carried it out despite all the hardships it entailed. He obeyed God when he was called to leave his relatives and his homeland, walking after Him without knowing where he was going (Heb. 11:8). His commitment reached its zenith when he was willing to offer his only son as a burnt offering.

Jephthah the Gileadite was another example of commitment. He made a vow to God and carried it out (Judges 11:34,35).

Contrary to Abraham and Jephthah was Samson, who did not

abide by his vow. Rather, he forfeited his soul, lost his strength, was taken captive by his enemies, and became an example (Judges 16).

❈ Commitment to Covenants, Vows and Oaths ❈

A spiritual person commits to his covenants with the Lord, have you fulfilled all your covenants with God?

The first covenant between you and God took place on the day of your baptism; the covenant to renounce Satan and all his tricks, evilness, unclean spirits, and wicked deeds. Do you still adhere to this pledge? In every repentance and confession, you undertake before God a vow to abandon sin without return, but do you abide by it? In every Holy Communion, you undertake many promises, but do you remember them? Have you carried them out? Or have you abandoned them?

How many times have you suffered from severe tribulations and vowed before God that if He saves you, you will do such and such? Do you abide by the pledges which you vow before God during your affliction? Behold David the Prophet says, "I will pay my vows to the Lord now in the presence of all His people" (Psa. 115:8). Are you like this? Are you devoted to all your vows? Or do you renege, change your mind, postpone paying your vow, or disregard it?

Do you commit yourself to what you say in your prayers? In every prayer you say, "Forgive us our trespasses as we forgive those who trespass against us." Do you truly forgive others as you say, or do you not commit yourself to the words you pray? Review what you say in your prayers, put them into practice, and see where you stand. How many New Year Eves have passed in which you stood before God and made vows and promises? How many spiritual moments has your heart burnt with repentance and made promises and vows to God, but you adhered to none of them?

Your state resembles these lines:

How many times have I promised God, yet breached?
O, I should not have promised for I am weak.

❈ Lack of Commitment ❈

Lack of commitment often points to a spirit of apathy and recklessness. It reveals a person who is devoid of any sense of responsibility. It is a proof of weakness, appearing at the beginning of creation when our forefathers did not adhere to the commandment they received from God and were driven out of Paradise. We have seen the adversities which have befallen mankind due to this failure of adhering to a commitment.

The children of Israel also failed in their commitment. When Moses presented them with the Ten Commandments, they all cried out to him saying, "Tell us all that the Lord our God says to you, and we will hear and do it" (Deu. 5:27). Were they dedicated to this pledge? Did they not, soon after worship the golden calf (Ex. 32)? Has any generation of mankind adhered to this declaration? How wonderful is the saying of David the Prophet: "Accept, I pray, the freewill offerings of my mouth, O Lord" (Psa. 118:108)! When you pray these words, do you mean them? Do you mean what you are saying, which is, "Give me, O Lord, a spirit of commitment that I may carry out all my pledges and not break my vows?"

If we feel the need to commit to our agreements with people out of a spirit of obligation, how much more should we be committed to our agreements with God? He who fails to commit tries to cover his failure with many excuses and justifications in order to evade his responsibility. He may make excuses of hindrances and obstacles, claiming that the matter was beyond his will and ability, that the circumstances were unfavorable, that he had forgotten, or that he had no time. However, in most cases, the true reason is that he is not used to a life of commitment and respect to his word.

On the other hand, a committed spiritual person exerts every effort to overcome any obstacles or difficulties he may encounter, fulfilling his commitments as a responsible person. In fact, he would despise himself if he presented an excuse to be exempted from any agreement. That is why you feel comfortable dealing with someone recognized for his commitment. You feel assured that you are walking on safe ground and certain that he will produce sound results, so you sleep peacefully, confident that you are working with a man who appreciates the situation and respects his agreements.

On the other hand, he who is not committed follows his whims, he does not heed orders or regulations and tries to loosen himself from everything he deems restrictive. He does not fulfil any commitments in his worldly or spiritual life. He may even refuse to submit to public rules, demanding his personal freedom and disregarding any laws or regulations that "freedom" may violate. Such a person does not comprehend the true meaning of freedom. He believes rules are restrictions constraining his freedom of opinion and will. True freedom, however, is freedom from the lusts, desires, and habits that enslave us.

When a person detaches himself from commitment in the name of freedom, society is obliged to compel him. Thus, by abandoning commitment, he faces compulsion. He becomes constrained by laws and penalties and in need of inspection, supervision, and control by society. If he persists in his non-adherence, he is compelled against his will to fulfill his commitments. His obedience becomes a submission to compulsion rather than a love for commitment.

Nevertheless, some, in the spiritual and ecclesiastical sphere, may ask: What is the need for commitment when we are under grace and not under the law? Grace does not conflict with commitment. He who through grace has risen above the law's requirements, has no obligation, but he who has not, continues to submit to the law. Let us take the tithes as an example. A person is no longer obligated by the law to pay his tithes if he, conforming to the principles, of almsgiving, pays even more. He abides by the commands to give to those who ask, and to sell one's possessions and give to the poor. This is the level of grace, if you have not yet attained it, you are committed to the law of tithes.

Similarly, some may object to the seven daily prayers. Unless you have reached the level of unceasing, continuous prayer in your life, you are still obligated to the daily prayers, for reciting them will teach you the life of prayer.

Brethren, may we all live a life of commitment, for it embraces within it the life of obedience and the life of humility. It also includes seriousness, meticulousness, and the fear of God, because all virtues are related to each other.

❈ Characteristics of a Committed Person ❈

A committed person respects himself and his word, his promises, and his relationships with others. His commitment breeds confidence in him as well as in his work and behavior. Such a person is dependable, trustworthy, supportive, and appreciated by all. A committed person can withstand obstacles and overcome hindrances in order to carry out what was commended to him, even if this causes him pressure or hardship. Thus, he performs his work with proficiency. He is always prosperous because he sees the performance and success of his work as part of his values, honor, and self-respect, and any negligence as an embarrassment to him and everyone who works with him.

In addition to his social life, a committed person adheres to commitments in both his private and spiritual life as well. He abides by every spiritual practice that he lays down or that is laid down by his spiritual father for his benefit. He commits himself to his ascetic practices and spiritual canon of prayer, fasting, prostrations, and spiritual readings without deviation, cutbacks, or excuses for his shortcomings. A committed person does not find in external circumstances a justification for his non-adherence. His seriousness in life makes him an example and a lesson to others, unlike an uncommitted person who causes others to stumble when they imitate his way of life.

He who commits himself is vigilant over his energy so that he may be able to fulfill his obligations. He is cautious over his time so as not to disturb his services or arrangements, and to perfect any work he is committed to perform. He does not waste his effort, strength, or time in trivial matters and amusements, for doing so would prevent him from fulfilling those obligations.

He who is committed does not forget any of his commitments, for he does not allow forgetfulness to be an excuse for his shortcomings. He records his responsibilities and frequently reviews them to avoid any negligence.

He also serves with a spirit of commitment, an attribute of every successful minister. He abides by the time of his service; he does not skip days or arrive late, and by the program or curriculum; he does not deviate from it or innovate a special one for himself. He does not fail to adhere to preparing the lesson, making his prior knowledge of it an alibi, rather he ensures it is rich and satisfying to his listeners every time. He attends all servants' meetings and submits to the discipline of service in every aspect.

A spiritual servant commits himself to time. If he is invited to give a sermon for one hour, he does not take two hours, unheeding the time of the congregation and their private appointments. He also adheres to the subject of the sermon and does not waste time on unrelated or irrelevant issues. Thus, the committed servant is meticulous in everything, even the time and subject matter.

Commitment is an important element in the life of priests and clergymen. They are obliged to perform the responsibilities of their canonical work; liturgical services, visitations to all the congregation, appointments for confession, and visiting the sick and distressed. They are committed to their responsibilities towards the poor and needy and to presenting themselves as role models in every virtue. A priest who is uncommitted has no specific duties set before him, he acts in whichever way is pleasing to him, adhering to nothing, and following no plan or discipline.

Commitment also affects the realm of doctrine and dogma. Every person who stands at the pulpit to teach should adhere to the teachings of the Holy Bible and the doctrines of the Church. He should not present his listeners with his own opinions or beliefs, or his personal conclusions from his readings. Rather, he should teach according to the words of the Holy Bible and the Tradition of the Church. To this effect, Saint Paul said to his disciple, Bishop Timothy, "And the things that you have heard from me among many witnesses, commit these to faithful men who will be able to teach others also" (2 Tim. 2:2).

A spiritual person is bound to the teachings of the Church and to Her decrees, rituals, fastings, prayers, and canons. He should not stray away from the path of the Church, for in the commitment of all, there is oneness of heart and of thought, of worship and of faith.

That is why the life of humility befits the life of commitment. A humble person submits to regulations, whereas the haughty interprets matters according to his own understanding.

CHAPTER 9

Wisdom and Discernment

❧ The Importance of Wisdom and Discernment ❧

Saint Antony, the Father of the monks, was once asked, "Which is the greatest of all virtues?" He answered, "Discernment is undoubtedly the greatest."[1]

(Conferences 2.2)

Discernment is a person's ability to differentiate between right and wrong and between good and evil. Many people fast, pray, confess, partake of the Holy Communion, and read the Holy Bible, yet fail in their spiritual life because they have no discernment. They practice all these things without any wisdom or insight. Every spiritual exercise or virtue should be practiced with

---

[1] St. John Cassian in his Conferences writes the following story of St. Antony: Some elders came to St. Antony and asked him, "Which is the greatest of all virtues?" Each one then gave an opinion, some saying that "fasting and keeping of vigils" best help one come near to God; others said "voluntary poverty" and "detachment"; others said "compassion." Last of all, St. Anthony gave his reply: "All that you have said is both necessary and helpful for those who are searching for God and wish to come to Him. But we cannot award the first place to any of these virtues; for there are many among us who have endured fasting and vigils, or have withdrawn into the desert, or have practiced poverty to such an extent that they have not left themselves enough for their daily sustenance, or have performed acts of compassion so generously that they no longer have anything to give; and yet these same monks, having done all this, have nevertheless fallen away miserably from virtue and slipped into vice. What was it, then, that made them stray from the straight path? In my opinion, it was simply that they did not possess the grace of discrimination [discernment]; for it is this virtue that teaches a man to walk along the royal road, swerving neither to the right through immoderate [excessive] self-control, nor to the left through indifference and laxity. Discrimination is a kind of eye and lantern of the soul, as is said in the Gospel passage: 'The light of the body is the eye; if therefore your eye is pure, your whole body will be full of light. But if your eye is evil, your whole body will be full of darkness' (Matt. 6:22-3). And this is just what we find. For the power of discrimination, scrutinizing all the thoughts and actions of a man, distinguishes and sets aside everything that is base and not pleasing to God, and keeps him free from delusion....Scripture also refers to it as discernment without which we must do nothing—not even drink the spiritual wine that 'makes glad the heart of man' (Psa. 104:15), for it is said, 'Drink with discernment' (Prov. 31:3), and 'he that does not do all things with discernment is like a city that is broken down and without walls' (Prov. 25:28). Wisdom, intellect and perceptiveness are united in discrimination; and without these our inner house cannot be built, nor can we gather spiritual wealth (cf. Prov. 24:3-4)...These passages show very clearly that without the gift of discrimination no virtue can stand or remain firm to the end, for it is the mother of all the virtues and their guardian."

wisdom. A person should first seek to understand its meaning and essence, then know how and when to practice it. In this way, discernment can penetrate every virtue.

The Holy Bible tells us, "The wise man's eyes are in his head, but the fool walks in darkness" (Ecc. 2:14). The Lord Jesus Christ emphasized the importance of wisdom many times, praising even the unjust steward because he had dealt wisely (Lk.16:8). Regarding the importance of walking in wisdom, the Lord said, "Be wise as serpents and harmless as doves" (Matt. 10:16).

Such is the wise conduct of all the children of God in life and in service. We see Saint Peter the Apostle praising the wisdom with which Saint Paul the Apostle preached, saying, "As also our beloved brother Paul, according to the wisdom given to him, has written to you" (2 Pet. 3:15).

Wisdom was a necessary qualification in the election of ministers to the rank of deacon. In choosing the seven deacons, our fathers the Apostles said, "Therefore, brethren, seek out from among you seven men of good reputation, full of the Holy Spirit and wisdom, whom we may appoint over this business" (Acts 6:3).

❈ Wisdom is One of the Names of Christ ❈

Owing to its importance, wisdom is one of the titles of the Second Person of the Holy Trinity. The Apostle speaks of Christ the Lord, saying He is "the power of God and the wisdom of God" (1 Cor. 1:24), "in Whom are hidden all the treasures of wisdom and knowledge" (Col. 2:3). It is also written in the Book of Proverbs, "Wisdom has built her house, She has hewn out her seven pillars" (Prov. 9:1), which are the Seven Holy Mysteries of the Church.

❈ Wisdom and the Holy Spirit ❈

He, in whom the Spirit of God dwells, is no doubt a dwelling place for wisdom. For it is said of the Holy Spirit in the Book of

Isaiah the Prophet that He is the Spirit of the Lord, the Spirit of wisdom, the Spirit of understanding, and the Spirit of counsel (Isa. 11:2).

Saint Paul tells the Ephesians that the Holy Spirit is "the Spirit of wisdom and revelation in the knowledge of Him," Whom, if they received, would enlighten the eyes of their understanding (Eph. 1:17,18). The Apostle also says that wisdom is one of the gifts of the Holy Spirit (1 Cor. 12:8).

❈ The Wisdom of God and the Wisdom of the World ❈

We must differentiate between the wisdom of God and the cunning of the world, for it is said He "catches the wise in their own craftiness" (1 Cor. 3:19). Saint Paul explained in great detail the difference between the wisdom of God and the wisdom of the world which will be destroyed (1 Cor. 1:19), and said that "the wisdom of this world is foolishness with God" (l Cor. 3:19). He called this second type, "the wisdom of men" (1 Cor. 2:5), the wisdom "according to the flesh" (1 Cor. 1:26), and "the wisdom of this age (l Cor. 2:6). He added that "God has chosen the foolish things of the world to put to shame the wise" (1 Cor. 1:27).

However, in regards to spiritual wisdom—which is from God and His Spirit—St. Paul said: "However, we speak wisdom among those who are mature, yet not the wisdom of this age, nor of the rulers of this age, who are coming to nothing. But we speak the wisdom of God in a mystery. the hidden wisdom which God ordained before the ages for our glory" (1 Cor. 2:6,7). Saint James the Apostle also said that the wisdom which is from God is the wisdom which is "from above." He explained this in detail, saying: "But the wisdom that is from above is first pure, then peaceable, gentle, willing to yield, full of mercy and good fruits, without partiality and without hypocrisy" (James 3:17). He differentiates between this spiritual wisdom and that of this world, which he described as "earthly, sensual, demonic" (James 3:15), saying "where envy and self-seeking exist, confusion and every evil thing" (James 3:16).

The wisdom of the world is full of craftiness and cunning. With lies and deception as its means, it has many cracks from which Satan can enter. It was in this manner that the serpent, which was "more cunning than any beast of the field" (Gen. 3:1), behaved when it deceived our mother Eve. Similarly, Jezebel—the wife of the evil King Ahab—devised an immoral scheme for her husband to possess the vineyard of Naboth the Jezreelite (1 Kin. 21:5-15). Likewise, our mother Rebekah behaved with worldly wisdom in order to obtain for her son, Jacob, the blessing of his father. Even Jacob feared her lies, deception, and cunning and said to her, "I shall bring a curse on myself and not a blessing" (Gen. 27:12).

Not every means that allows you to accomplish your goal is sound and proper. The means of the world may be quicker to take you to your aim, but they are unacceptable before God. Our father Abraham took Keturah as his wife, and she begot Zimran, Jokshan, Medan, Midian, Ishbak, and Shuah who gave birth to Sheba, Dedan, Asshurim, Letushim, and Leummim and others (Gen.25:1-4). Yet, those children were not accepted before God, for they were the result of human means.

Another example of human wisdom which was not acceptable to God was the counsel of Ahithophel. It was human intelligence which brought about a result, but this was an evil intelligence such that virtuous people prayed that the Lord would deliver them from (2 Sam. 15:31). The counsel which Balaam presented to Balak (Rev. 2:14) is another example. Likewise, the tricks of the devil which have misled many and will mislead more in the last days, for it is diabolic wisdom as our teacher Saint James the Apostle describes (James 3:15).

We have to avoid worldly means and reject their outcome, even if they seem favorable to us. No matter what thoughts the devil or our human intelligence claim to be beneficial for us, let us reject them, for their means are unsound and unspiritual. The Holy

Bible warns us saying, "There is a way that seems right to a man, but its end is the way of death" (Prov.14:12); (Prov. 16:25).

❈ Sources of Wisdom ❈

Our first source of wisdom is God, through our prayers. As the Apostle says, "If any of you lacks wisdom, let him ask of God, who gives to all liberally and without reproach, and it will be given to him. But let him ask in faith, with no doubting" (James 1:5,6). Therefore, we constantly pray to God to guide us, enlighten our hearts and minds, grace us with wisdom, and teach us how to walk in His path. Since wisdom is from above (James 3), let us then seek it from above.

The second source of wisdom is the counsel of people through whom God speaks. Concerning this, the Apostle Saint Paul says, "Remember those who rule over you, who have spoken the word of God to you, whose faith follow... Obey those who rule over you, and be submissive, for they watch out for your souls, as those who must give account" (Heb. 13:7-17). How truthful is the saying, "those who have no guidance fall like the leaves ¨ (cf. Prov. 11:12, LXX)!

The third source of wisdom is wise and experienced people. A poet says about this, "If you must send a messenger as a diplomatic messenger, send a wise man and do not give him orders. But if some matter is complex for you, seek the counsel of a prudent one and do not disobey him."[2] Thus, it is not enough to seek the counsel of wise people, but also to submit and obey them.

The poet also said, "Take knowledge from those who possess it and wisdom from the wise." This refers to the importance of choosing a good spiritual guide from whom one can acquire wisdom. Saint Antony, at the beginning of his monastic life, sought counsel from the ascetics and was like the bee, sucking nectar from every flower. Many are those who seek wisdom from

---

[2] John William Sutton, ed. The Dictes and Sayings of the Philosophers |p248 |r10-11, Dicts. Ahiqar Syr Camb Add 2020, no.41 = Syr Berlin 165, no.38. Similarly, Syr Ber- lin 134, no.47; Arm A, no.65; Arm B,no.116; Slav, no.50) See also Prov 13:17

one person and become a carbon copy of them, but Saint Antony learned asceticism from one person, prayer from a second one, meekness from a third, cheerfulness from a fourth, knowledge from a fifth, etc.

❈ The Most Important Area where Wisdom is Necessary ❈

Deeds can be divided into four categories. Some deeds are clearly good; others are clearly evil. Both of these require no discernment. The third type are those deeds that leave a person unsure whether it is good or evil and hesitant of its means and outcome. This type requires intelligence and discernment, or at least good

counseling and words of wisdom to enlighten one's way. This type of deeds highlight the importance of spiritual fathers and spiritual guides.

The last type is a deed that demands a choice between two options, with the better choice unclear. Both options may be good, but which is better or more suitable is unknown. An example of this is when a person does not know whether to consecrate his life by means of monastic life or the service of the priesthood. Both options are good, but which is better for that specific person? Which one is more suitable for his particular personality? Such matters need wisdom, discernment, and time for the person to examine himself and hear the voice of God either in his heart, through the mouth of a wise father, or through a sincere guide.

Wisdom and discernment are also needed when acquiring or advancing in a virtue. For while virtues are clearly explained in many spiritual books, the means to acquire them may remain ambiguous. Rushing to acquire a virtue can yield opposite results or spiritual relapses; and moving too slowly can result in lukewarmness, procrastination, or stagnation. The mind may falter between the fervor of hastiness and the slackness of the gradual approach, asking "What do I do?"

We cannot assume that hastiness or slowness is always better.

One should not tarry during instances of a strong impulse or stirring up of the Grace of the Holy Spirit. This is what happened with Saint Abba Mishael the hermit, Saints Maximous and Domadius, and others like them who attained virtues quickly. In other cases, however, gradual advancing may be more suitable.

Furthermore, discernment is necessary in matters that seem sensitive or fateful. Acting without wisdom can cause a person to commit mistakes that he will regret all his life or that are costly to his future. Lamenting for the rest of his life will be to no avail. Thus, the matter requires caution, wisdom, and guidance.

In other cases, a person may be passionate about a decision, investing all his emotions in it, but that passion later proves to be unfavorable. That person will regret his decision and blame himself saying, "I wish I had not done that…I wish I had waited, sought guidance, or listened to the advice I passionately rejected." Such a matter required discernment and a detailed examination into the various options, aspects and outcomes of the decision. Therefore, counseling not only presents different aspects and gives insight into ambiguous details, but it also helps bring to light potential outcomes that may have been overlooked.

There is another essential point that demands discernment and wisdom, that is the acquisition of virtues in a balanced manner.

❈ Wisdom is the Basis for Proper Understanding ❈

Some people often regret forgiving certain people in humility, when it results in emotional suffering or mockery. But the problem in these cases is not with a life of humility, but the application of humility without discernment or understanding. Such people need to understand the true meaning of humility and practice it with wisdom and discernment to avoid such distress. They should situate humility in their hearts so as not to resort to violence or cling to pride following a bad experience.

There are many virtues that, if practiced without discernment or with impulsiveness, could lead to unexpected results, deviation from sound spirituality, or psychological distress. To practice what is written in *The Paradise of the Fathers* or other spiritual books and discourses that reference high spiritual levels and ideals requires guidance, discernment, and wisdom. Do not read about virtues that a saintly person acquired after decades of strife and decide to apply what you read right then and there, without gradual progress, discernment, and wisdom.

This advice covers many virtues, such as:

† Silence and solitude

† Fasting, abstaining from food, and successive abstinence for days

† Humility and taking the last seat

† Tears and contrition of heart

† The meaning of cheerfulness and dejection

† Continual prayer

† The meaning of judging and counseling

† Meekness and strength of personality

† Forgiveness, strictness, and discipline

† Asceticism and self-control

† Defending the Truth

† Obedience and freedom of conscience

❈ Intelligence and Wisdom ❈

True wisdom comes from above as one of the gifts of the Holy Spirit. It differs from any alleged human or worldly wisdom which is not from God. Some people may consider shrewdness, tactfulness, and diplomacy as wisdom. The same for those who are sly or clever. All these are far from true wisdom which comes "from above" (James 3). Here we would like to differentiate between intelligence and wisdom.

Wisdom is much broader than intelligence; intelligence is a mere fragment of wisdom. A person may possess extraordinary intelligence yet does not behave wisely. Obstacles may hinder his thinking and intellectual abilities from practical behavior. One obstacle can be the command of a certain lust over him. If he succumbs to lust's control of his behavior, he may behave without wisdom, for the lust has impeded his intelligence and taken over his reins. Another obstacle is maybe emotions which overtakes one's actions, making them irrational. Here, even though one's intellect is intact, that person does not possess the necessary experience or knowledge to make wise decisions. What, then, is wisdom and how is it different from intelligence?

The source of intelligence is the mind and the healthy activities of the brain. Wisdom, however, stems from sound reasoning and practical decision-making. It does not depend solely on the brain, but also on experience, guidance, prayer, and direction from the Holy Spirit. Therefore, wisdom is not merely knowledge or proper thinking, it is an essential component of daily life, conveyed in good conduct, rather than theoretical or intellectual information.

How true are the words of Saint James the Apostle, "Who is wise and understanding among you? Let him show by good conduct that his works are done in the meekness of wisdom" (James 3:13). Indeed, sound reasoning, or intelligence, enters a thorough test in practical situations. If it succeeds, it becomes wisdom.

An intelligent person who, nonetheless, lacks the knowledge of the proper meaning of words will lack precision in his expression. But, a wise person expresses what he means and means what he expresses. Thus, wisdom consists of good reasoning, accurate expression, and sound behavior.

Every wise person is intelligent, but not every intelligent person is wise. If a wise person lacks intelligence, he compensates for this by obtaining guidance, reading, benefiting from his own and others' experiences, as well as from history. Like the poet says, "Whoever has the knowledge of history in his heart, has added many ages to his age."

The importance of experience as a component of wisdom gave rise to the term "the wisdom of the elders." This means that, during their lifetime, the elders encountered various experiences that gave them wisdom irrespective of their level of intelligence. Wise guides add sound reasoning to the minds of those whom they counsel, presenting them with new points of view which have gone unnoticed due to the lack of experience and limited perception of their disciples. Such guidance and counsel prevent them from acting rashly in pursuit of the desires of the heart. For rashness can hinder intelligence or bend it towards a certain direction.

That is why, however intelligent you are, always remember the words of the Holy Bible, "lean not on your own understanding" (Prov. 3:5). Your understanding is constrained by the limits of your own knowledge, experience, and perspectives. Therefore, expand these to include the dimensions, outlooks, and experiences of others through counseling and guidance. A wise person is not rash in his conduct, but withholds his own opinion until he attains a deeper and broader perception.

❊ Hindrances to Wisdom ❊

Hastiness

Hastiness in conduct is a hindrance to wisdom. Hence, wise people are patient. Hastiness deters reflection, sound thinking, or analysis of different opinions. It does not allow a person to seek counsel, or guidance from God through prayer.

Hastiness also reflects superficiality. Hasty behavior is often frivolous and chaotic. God sends such people someone to advise them, saying, "Be on your guard. Take heed to yourself. Give yourself a chance to think. Review the matter with yourself."

Some of our children in the Lands of Immigration come to Egypt desiring to get married within a week or two. In contrast, when Saint Macarios the Great thought of going into the inner wilderness to see the anchorite fathers, we discover him saying, "I kept wrestling this thought for three years to see whether it was from God or not."

Wise people are prudent and balanced. They tend to delve deep into their thoughts and studies, examining them carefully even if it prolongs their process. We do not deny that some matters need a quick decision. But, there is a difference between expedience and rashness. Rashness is quickness without inspection or examination, which can be perilous for fateful matters. I always say, "The right solution is not the quick solution, but the perfected solution."

We often observe hastiness in youth. With their enthusiasm they like to expedite matters. However, discoursing with their elders may convince them of the dangers of hastiness. To other people, hastiness is a natural quality. These people need to train themselves to slow down and take time to think.

Frequently, people regret their rash actions because it caused them to err or treat others unjustly. An example of this is a reporter who hastens to publish a news story to get a "scoop" or a promotion. If later the story proves to be untrue, this reporter may cause people to lose their trust in the accuracy of the news. Another example is a father who punishes his child or a manager who fires an employee for some error, but later discover they misjudged and punished those who were innocent.

Lack of Knowledge

Other hindrances to wisdom are misunderstanding or lack of knowledge.

A man may be very intelligent yet fails in his marital life for his lack of knowledge of the psychology of the woman, treating his wife as he treats his male friends. A wise man studies the mentality and psychology of women so as to deal with them wisely. Likewise, a woman should study the psychology of man and his mentality to understand how to deal with him in wisdom. The same advice applies to the treatment of children; we should study the psychology of the child in order to treat them wisely.

This is recommended for all people. We should study the psychology, mentality, and characteristics of the people we deal with—whether they are our colleagues, managers, subordinates, friends, or neighbors—in order to deal with them in a proper way. If you do so, you will discover the keys by which you can unlock their hearts and succeed in your relationship with them. Even if at times the keys malfunction, you will possess the knowledge necessary to repair them and reopen their hearts.

Sometimes our failure in dealing with certain people is due more to our ignorance of how to treat them, than to their personal faults. That is why we need to examine some points about dealing with people.

❊ Wisdom in Silence and Speaking ❊

Many spiritual people practice the virtue of silence to avoid the sins of the tongue. They try to follow the words of the Holy Bible, "In the multitude of words sin is not lacking, but he who restrains his lips is wise" (Prov. 10:19), and those of David the Prophet, "Set a guard, O Lord, over my mouth; keep watch over the door of my lips" (Ps. 141:3). They repeat the words of the great Saint Arsenius, "Many times have I spoken and regretted, but I have never regretted my silence." Nevertheless, a wise person knows that not all silence is virtuous, nor all speaking sinful.

A wise person does not keep silent when he should speak and does not speak when he should keep silent. By wisdom, he knows when, how, and in what manner he should speak, such that he is praised like the bride in the Song of Songs; "Your lips, O my spouse, drip as honeycomb; honey and milk are under your tongue" (Song 4:11). A wise person speaks beneficial words, words of comfort and wisdom. Those who listen to him hear the Spirit of his Father speaking through him (Matt. 10:20). He speaks cautiously, gently, wisely, and usefully, he does not regret any word he says and does not long for a silence to protect him from the sins of the tongue.

The matter, then, needs discernment. Silence should not be taken as a strict ascetic practice void of Spirit because in some cases, silence is wrong. The wise person knows how to behave when faced with foolishness from people, whereas another person finds himself bewildered between two verses: "Do not answer a fool according to his folly, lest you also be like him" (Prov. 26:4) and "Answer a fool according to his folly, lest he be wise in his own eyes" (Prov. 26:5). However, there is no contradiction between these two verses. With wisdom, a person knows when to answer a fool and when not to answer him, for if your answer will make you equally as foolish, then it is better for you to keep silent and not answer, but if your silence will make him wise in his own eyes, it is better to reveal to him the foolishness of his words.

Wisdom is the deciding factor in the matter and through discernment you can determine which of the two ways is better. It is unreasonable to give one rule for all cases, we cannot say that you should keep silent when one word from you can solve a problem or when your silence can be misinterpreted for something other than what you intended. In like manner, we cannot say that you should speak in all circumstances. A person should not read what is written in *The Paradise of the Fathers* and apply it without first seeking advice as he is not a monk and his spiritual circumstances are different from those of monks.

At times, silence can signify discretion, wisdom, and avoidance of errors, it can be a realm for contemplation and prayer. But at other times, it can signify ignorance, laziness, foolishness, or fear and unmanly behavior. Discernment helps us distinguish between both cases. Thus, a spiritual guide should not burden his disciple with commandments that he may see as aimless, rather he should give him wisdom and discernment and leave him to behave the way he deems fit. What we say about silence applies to the other virtues as well.

❈ Wisdom in Mourning and Joy ❈

Some people start their spiritual life with repentance, weeping over their sins. As it is said in the The Paradise of the Fathers, they adhere to the verse, "For by a sad countenance the heart is made better" (Ecc. 7:3). However, they persist in this state to the extent that sorrow becomes a fixed feature of their life. Remembering how the Lord blessed those who mourn (Matt. 5:4), they put before them the virtue of "tears" which springs from contrition of heart.

Tears can be a sign of repentance and an indication of tender feelings and sensitivity, signifying asceticism and death to the world. Nevertheless, such a person needs great discernment lest his tears lead him in a contrary direction. Continuous sorrow and lack of wisdom, when accompanied with tears, can lead to various sins and errors. Let us explore some of these.

It is easy for sorrow to turn into a stumbling block, repelling those who wish to approach a life with God as they see religious life as nothing but weeping and depression. This is a distorted picture about life with God. For God desires our life with Him to be entirely and endlessly joyous. The Apostle describes it saying, "Rejoice in the Lord always. Again I will say, rejoice!" (Phil. 4:4). For, joy is a fruit of the Holy Spirit (Gal. 5:22).

The devil may also take advantage of a person's sorrow to throw him into despair and despondency. Sorry may weaken his morale, induce boredom or provoke resentment. Thus, a wise person realizes the limit to contrition and tears. He knows how to mingle them with hope and consolation. He lives a life of joy through his repentance, contrition, and tears which are shed in secret. These tears are comforting tears, not those of suffering...

❈ Wisdom and Spiritual Discernment ❈

The Spiritual life is not simply following laws, regulations and statutes; it is the establishment of the soul in God, with love and freedom. For example, a person may decide to avoid laughter for a week to avoid lukewarmness. If he takes his exercise in a literal sense, he will remain frowning and serious during any happy occasions during the week. This may negatively impact his relationships with others. Is that, then, steadfastness in a spiritual exercise or a lack of discernment?

Spiritual practices should not be dry, literal, or void of comprehension; nor should they be constraining like bonds or chains. He who walks wisely in the spiritual life knows whether to take an action or its opposite for the sake of God and according to the circumstances, as our teacher Saint Paul mentioned concerning his own practices, "Everywhere and in all things I have learned both to be full and to be hungry, both to abound and to suffer need" (Phil. 4:12).

The children of God comprehend the Spirit of life, not mere phrases and letters. They know which action to take with a clear conscience as the Holy Bible says, "Rejoice with those who rejoice, and weep with those who weep" (Rom. 12:15). For there is a time for everything under Heaven, as the Book of Ecclesiastes says, "a time for weeping, a time for laughter, a time for keeping silence and a time for speaking" (Ecc. 3:1-8).

Everything should be done in the proper time, in the appropriate manner, and with wisdom. A wise person does the appropriate thing at the right time without having to constrain himself to a certain condition for the rest of his life.

❈ Wisdom in Reading and Applying Holy Scripture ❈

A wise person does not take one verse from the Holy Bible and apply it to his life in its literal sense. Rather, he uses it in its right time and knows when to add to it other verses to clarify its meaning. We previously gave the example of mourning and joy. Let us expand upon this now.

Sometimes, people learn and benefit from a person's tears as they recognize his spirituality, care for his salvation, and tender feelings. At other times, however, having a sad countenance makes people worry and doubt. That is why many spiritual leaders keep their tears private and choose to appear cheerful before people. They do this out of care for people's feelings lest by their worry they make them worry. Thus, their cheerfulness brings joy to others.

I was highly pleased with the words of the writer who said: "How noble is the sad heart who would sing a joyous song with joyous hearts."[3] Thus, it is not wise for a person to lay down for himself a spiritual exercise and practice it without discernment or heed to the surrounding circumstances because this may result in many problems.

Some people read and apply what they read literally. This makes them grow weary and oftentimes, relapse.

Someone who reads *The Paradise of the Fathers* and applies what he read in a literal manner is oblivious to two things. First, Paradise describes the high spiritual levels that were attained by saintly Fathers after extended periods of struggle. These levels are not fit for beginners.

Second, *Paradise* announces recommendations given by the Fathers to certain people whose circumstances are different than his own. Indeed, saintly fathers gave different advice to different people as they deem fit for each one of them. They do not give standard counsel to everyone. But we should select what suits us from our readings and practice it with proper discernment, guidance and progression. The same applies concerning the psalms. Some of the psalms are suitable for joy while some are suitable

---
[3] Khalil Gibran, "Sand and Foam."

for mourning. One should choose what corresponds to their state and apply it. Even though some of the psalms are of a high spiritual level, which you may not have attained, you can still pray them as models set before you.

For every spiritual book you read, pay attention to two things: (1) the spirit of the words and not their literal meaning; and (2) what suits you personally. By this I mean what suits your circumstances and your level, what suits your spiritual stature, what suits your capacity and capabilities, and what conforms with your gradual steps in God's path. It is very dangerous to apply what you read without discernment, wisdom, and guidance. Instead, we seek a peaceful spiritual life which grows, loves goodness, and walks with wisdom.

❧ Wisdom in Kindness and Strictness ❧

Some people use meekness and kindness alone, while others make strictness, power, and authority their way of life. Wisdom says: Use strictness when it is needed to resolve matters and meekness when it is more effective. In your meekness, do not be overly lenient in a way that tires you; and in your strictness do not be too harsh in a way that offends others.

The Lord Jesus Christ used both meekness and strictness. He was meek and humble of heart such that it was said of Him, "He will not quarrel nor cry out, nor will anyone hear His voice in the streets. A bruised reed He will not break, and a smoking flax He will not quench" (Matt. 12:19, 20). But He was also strict when rebuking the Scribes and Pharisees, saying to them, "Woe to you, hypocrites!" (Matt. 23). The Lord Jesus was strict even with His disciple St. Peter, and once rebuked him saying, "Get behind Me, Satan! You are an offense to Me, for you are not mindful of the things of God, but the things of men" (Matt. 16:23). Likewise, when Peter was embarrassed to let Him wash his feet, He said to him, "If I do not wash you, you have no part with Me" (John 13:8). To this extent, was our meek Lord was strict at times.

Therefore, there are situations that demand strictness. An example of this is when the Lord cleansed the Temple. We see the meek Lord—Who said to the sinful woman, "Neither do I condemn you; go and sin no more" (John 8:11) and saved her from the hands of those who were condemning her—drove out the sellers, made a whip of cords, overturned the tables of the moneychangers, and ordered people to take away the doves. Here, we find the Lord using different degrees of strictness, applying to every condition what was befitting. He overturned the tables of the moneychangers but did not overturn the tables of the doves. He rebuked some by His words, others he drove out, and for others He made a whip of cords. Therefore, everything was carried out with discernment and as required by the situation.

If you prefer meekness and kindness and observe someone acting in strictness, do not say, "I have been made to stumble, the ideals have shattered before my eyes." For, this is the danger of focusing on one virtue. The spiritual life does not consist of one virtue alone, and disregarding the rest; it is an integrated life with all the virtues intertwining to form one spiritual fabric.

In some situations, the lack of strictness is considered a sin, as in the case of Eli the Priest. God punished him severely and took the priesthood from his descendants because he was not strict in the upbringing of his children. It is true that Eli warned them of their error, but he did not restrain them and was lenient in chastening them (1 Sam. 3:12-14).

Thus, we are not astonished by the strictness with which Saint Peter dealt with Ananias and Sapphira, sentencing them to death without a chance to repent (Acts 5:1-11). At the time of its foundation, strictness was necessary for the edification of the Church so as to bar any idleness, treason, or lying from entering the Church. That is why it was said after their punishment, "So great fear came upon all the Church and upon all who heard these things" (Acts 5:11). Here, we observe an important point: Fear is sometimes as necessary as love, and there is no contradiction in this.

❧ Wisdom in Fear and Love ❧

The Holy Bible says, "The fear of the Lord is the beginning of wisdom" (Prov. 9:10). Therefore, fear (from a spiritual point of view) is not wrong, but rather a spiritual stage. He who does not fear winds up with a life of carelessness and apathy, as was said about the unjust judge who "did not fear God nor regard man" (Luke 18:2).

At certain periods in life, fear may be necessary for the upbringing of children. A child who does not fear his parents may walk recklessly without restraint, becoming a cause of bitterness to them. Likewise, a student who does not fear his teachers turns into a disruptive person, wasting the time of his classmates and irritating his instructors. However, fear is a stage that develops and transforms into love and reverence. Fathers and teachers should not blame themselves when they reprimand a son or a student, they should not say in themselves nor in their confession that they have sinned because they lost their meekness. On the contrary, their conscience should blame them if they are not strict when strictness was needed.

Wisdom outlines the limits of reprimanding, that it should spring from a person in a position of authority and be in a genuine, spiritual way. Saint Paul the Apostle was obliged to rebuke the Galatians who began with the Spirit and tried to be made perfect by the flesh (Gal.3:3). Holy zeal sometimes compels a person to become like a burning fire, which is why a spiritual person needs to understand where meekness stands in regard to zeal. Meekness and zeal is a lengthy topic, but we will mention one thing: everything under the heavens has its season (Ecc. 3:1). A person can behave zealously without losing his meekness, for he who loses his holy zeal through his misunderstanding of meekness errs. Thus, we have to understand meekness properly so that we do not think that it is laxity in disposition or stagnancy.

Some people see Elijah as a model of holy zeal and Jeremiah as that of meekness and tears. But Jeremiah the Prophet was also a model of zeal and defending the truth, not only a man of tears, and he who reads the Book of Jeremiah perceives that. David the Prophet was a model of courage, strength, and zeal, but at the same time, he was a man of repentance who drenched his bed with his tears (Psalm 6) and wept over the deaths of Absalom, Saul, and Jonathan.

However, the misplaced compassion of a mother can spoil her child. Such mothers are not wise and lack discernment. They must understand the true meaning of compassion, its extent, and its connection with sound upbringing and with the spiritual life of her child. The heavenly Father loved His Only Son, nevertheless, He sacrificed Him for our sake, and on the Cross "it pleased Him to bruise Him; He has put Him to grief" as a sin offering for our sake, and "has laid on Him the iniquity of us all" (Isa. 53:1-6). A wise physician knows when to recommend painkillers and tranquilizers, when to use the scalpel, and when to perform an amputation.

The subject of discernment involves the whole spiritual life, so if we talk about it we will talk about all virtues so what we have mentioned thus far is enough.

CHAPTER 10

Inner and Positive Work

❈ The Importance of Positive Work in Struggling Against Sin ❈

Every person, in edifying his spiritual life, is faced with two important aspects. The First is resisting sinning against other people to share in purifying the society he lives in. This is the life of struggle against sin and the devil, representing the negative side of the spiritual life. The second is the positive side of the spiritual life: life with God and the edification of the soul and spirit with virtues. It is tasting the sweetness of the love of God and enjoying communion with Him in a holy life.

The person who makes his whole life a struggle against sin undoubtedly suffers much. His life is consumed in fighting against sin, which the Holy Bible tells us "has cast down many wounded, and all who were slain by her were strong men" (Prov. 7:26). This person's life is also consumed in struggling against the devil who is a cruel, relentless and evil enemy. Having tried and tempted the human soul for thousands of years, he knows its weaknesses, its defects, and how to bring about its downfall.

Without question, this defensive work against sin is grueling and difficult. To spend life doing so is too exhausting for the soul to bear. The struggle against these evil powers is not an easy matter; for, although the devil lost his sanctity and purity, he did not lose his nature as an angel with capabilities and powers.

What then? Should a person leave the negative side and give up the struggle against sin? No, because this is assuredly submitting to sin, and the Apostle rebukes such people saying, "You have not yet resisted to bloodshed, striving against sin" (Heb. 12:4). Man should resist the devil, flesh, and sin with all his might and with all the grace that God gives him in order to remain steadfast until the last breath.

But the question is: Why is resisting sin so difficult? Why did many of the Fathers say that the beginning of the spiritual life is self-coercion and vanquishing of the self? This struggle will be difficult if it is void of positive work and mere struggle. "For the flesh lusts against the Spirit, and the Spirit against the flesh; and these are contrary to one another" (Gal. 5:17). But why this struggle? Because the love of God has not yet entered the heart and has not settled there. How does the love of God enter the heart? It enters through positive work.

❖ The Importance of Love for God ❖

Without positive work in the spiritual life resistance against sin would be a bitter and difficult task; and may also be unprofitable. We may ask, "Why does a person toil in his spiritual combats? Why does he often fluctuate between failure and success?" Because the love of God is not fully in his heart, he struggles in vain. He resists sin but cannot remain steadfast because he has neither the weapons to fight nor the strength to persevere. No doubt the strong weapon that can overcome sin is one's love for God. The love of God makes you abhor sin and say [with the righteous Joseph], "How then can I do this great wickedness, and sin against God?" (Gen. 39:9).

Sin, which causes you to suffer in your struggle against it and makes you fall and rise so often, will completely flee from your heart once the love of God enters. Once the love of God enters your heart, sin will have no power over you. You will need not exert great effort in your struggle against it, for your flesh will no longer work against your spirit. You will become naturally alienated from sin and the devil will find no place for himself in your heart, as the Lord Jesus Christ said, "the ruler of this world is coming, and he has nothing in Me" (John 14:30).

You will need to struggle against sin as long as you have worldly lusts within you that cause you to fall, for the desires of the Spirit are resisted by the lusts of the flesh. As long as those lusts are in your heart, you will resist God and allow the devil to come into you. He enters into your soul with all his helpers, as into a house decorated, furnished, and ready to receive him. But if the love of God is in your heart, your house will be shielded against sin. Sin will find it difficult to attack your heart. Then, you will be able to sing with David the Prophet and say to your protected soul, "Praise the Lord, O Jerusalem! Praise your God, O Zion! For He has strengthened the bars of your gates; He has blessed your children within you" (Psa. 146:12-13).

The love of God weakens the attacks of sin because there is nothing within you that conforms to it. The doors of your heart have become shut before the devil. That love shields you and bears within you many children, which are the fruits of the Spirit, virtues and righteous deeds. That is why the Psalmist not only says that God has strengthened the bars of your gates, which addresses the negative side, but also that "He has blessed your children within you," which is the positive side of spiritual life. It is comfortable, easy, and joyful to the heart to strive, in a positive manner, for the sake of knowing God and growing in His love. It is completely different from the negative striving in which you struggle against sin and the devil.

The most delightful thing in the spiritual life is this positive striving, for it is the taste of God and a foretaste of His Kingdom, it is life with Him in the depth of His love. In it, you do not suffer from spiritual wars or conflict with sin because there is nothing within you that is agreeable to it. Do you think that a person falls into sin because sin is powerful, the stumbling blocks in the path are strong, and the devil is full of wiles and trickery? Of course not! It is more so that he falls because the love of God is not in his heart. If he loves God, he will not find sin attractive nor will he feel that it is powerful in its war against him; rather, he will loath it because it is incompatible with his pure nature.

❈ Attaining the Love of God ❈

A person can attain the love of God through positive spiritual work. Positive striving leads one to love God and this causes him not to sin because "Love never fails" (1 Cor. 13:8), as St. Paul said. St. John the Apostle also said: "God is love, and he who abides in love abides in God, and God in him" (1 John 4:16), and "he cannot sin, because he has been born of God" (1 John 3:9). Therefore, try to fill your heart with love for God. Then, His love inside you will be like a burning fire consuming all the lusts of sin together with all its residues and thoughts. What is this positive work that leads to this love?

Be mindful of God always. Your remembrance of Him will generate His love in your heart and His love will make you think more of Him. Each of these leads to and strengthens the other. If you increase your remembrance of God, heaven, His angels, His words, and commandments, if you contemplate on the eternal bliss with Him, His beautiful attributes, and how He deals with people, then you will be preoccupied with Him. Your preoccupation will make you remember Him more and your remembrance of Him will increase your love for Him, and so on, like a cycle.

Your remembrance of God is the first positive work in your spiritual life. God must be before you all time. You should always remember Him, as David said: "O, how I love Your law! It is my meditation all the day" (Psa.118:97). Your remembrance of God will sanctify your thoughts and generate spiritual feelings in your heart. This will make you feel ashamed to dwell on any wrong thought or to mingle your holy thoughts with any abominable or even worldly ideas. Your remembrance of God will lead you to purity of heart because there is no communion whatsoever between light and darkness (2 Cor. 6:14). You will become accustomed to prayer, contemplation, and meditation, feeling the presence of God at all times.

In God's Divine presence, the devil will not dare approach you. For even if he does, he will find no place for himself in you and will leave quickly. He will not find you ready for him, seeing that your ways do not agree with his. Even if he attempts to fight you, it will be a feeble temptation because you are immersed in God. Instead, he will concentrate his effort on keeping you away from your preoccupation with God rather than tempting you openly with sins.

If the devil succeeds in keeping you away from your positive work, he will proceed with his next step which is to make you relapse into your negative struggle. Nevertheless, even in this condition you will be able to resist his temptations, having acquired strength from your previous spiritual acts. He will be tempting you while respecting and fearing you, taking his guard against you and unable to use all his might. But the person who is far from the positive work is easy prey for the devils. They do not fear him because they know he lacks the strength from within to fight them.

In addition to the remembrance of God, spiritual reading is also very beneficial as a positive work to immerse the intellect in God. It provides a person with subjects for contemplation and prayer. It is like the raising of incense, preparing the altar for the oblations to be offered. Reading takes your thoughts to a spiritual atmosphere and brings to your remembrance God and His saints. The word of God is efficacious, it works in you, giving fervor to your spirituality and prompting you with ardor to the Lord's path. It enlightens your thoughts and generates in you spiritual feelings, strengthening your will to walk in God's path.

Similarly, spiritual gatherings are beneficial for uniting a person with God. They include prayers, readings, hymns, and spiritual songs and beneficial sayings. All these bring you to a spiritual atmosphere, from which the devil feels estranged.

Spiritual friendship is also very beneficial. It is a positive act which strengthens your heart and attracts you towards God. A spiritual friend is one who makes you remember God and His commandments, condemn yourself for your sins, and from whom you learn the life of virtue. Sin could not enter the life of Lot and his family when they were living with our father Abraham. But it found an opportunity when they distanced themselves from this spiritual friendship by living in Sodom. There, Lot was tormented with the sins of its inhabitants.

Finally, partaking of the Mystery of the Eucharist is one of the most important positive works for its deep efficacies on the soul and all that it entails from continual repentance and confession. The Lord Jesus Christ said of the person who partakes of the Holy Communion that he "abides in Me and I in him" (John 6:56). We also say in the Divine Liturgy, "We partake of Your Holy Mysteries for the sanctification of our souls, our bodies and our spirits."

What have you acquired of these spiritual works? And what spiritual practices by which you train yourself on the life of the Spirit and the fruit of the Spirit have you learned? Do you engage your daily thoughts on your eternity and its necessary deeds? What about giving an account of yourself for all your inadequacies and sins? What about keeping your prostrations, fasts, and conduct in the life of the Spirit?

❈ The Benefits of Positive Work ❈

Through all these positive works, you create within yourself an equilibrium between the impact of the world and that of the Spirit. If the devil approaches you to tempt you and finds you without the Bible, psalms, prayer, contemplation, spiritual meditation, spiritual gatherings, fasting, prostrations, confession, or Holy Communion, what state will you be in? How will you be able to resist sin without any weapon? You will then be like a city that is being attacked by the enemy without an army, weapons, or fortifications.

Take this precept and set it before you: Every person who falls into sin must have been away from positive work for a long time, whether it be the spiritual means of grace, the practice of virtue, or the love of God. In this manner, sin comes to a person when he is unprepared or in a state of weakness or lukewarmness. The Lord says, "And pray that your flight may not be in winter or on the Sabbath" (Matt. 24:20). Here, "winter" means in the time of spiritual coolness and "on the Sabbath" means during a time when you are without any work, both pointing to one's abandoning of positive spiritual work. Therefore, always be alert in your heart; let there be oil in your lamp. As the Lord said about readiness, "Let your waist be girded and your lamps burning" (Luke 12:35).

Concern yourself with spiritual work, for it grants you strength to resist sin. Fill your heart with spiritual things so that you may not be overcome by the years of poverty, with its famine and deficiency. Keep your stone in your sling, so that if Goliath appears before you, you may be able to go forward and say with confidence, "This day the Lord will deliver you into my hand" (1 Sam. 17:46). Do not limit your struggle to resisting the negatives because this will exhaust you. But also strive in the positive work which gives you the strength by which you can fight sin. May the Lord be with you.

❈ The Importance of Inner Work ❈

Spiritual life is not just outward practices performed by the body, its spiritual criterion depends on a person's spiritual state from within, with regard to his intentions, impulses, the movement of his heart, and the state of his mind.

We should not forget the saying of the Lord, "My son, give Me your heart" (Prov. 23:26), and "Keep your heart with all diligence, for out of it springs the issues of life" (Prov. 4:23). This means that virtue begins in the heart. They spring from the heart and are manifest in the person's deeds. Every good, external deed which does not spring from the heart is not considered virtue. The Lord rejected every worship offered to Him that did not come from a pure heart, which is why He rebuked the Jews saying, "This people honors Me with their lips, but their heart is far from Me" (Mark 7:6). Therefore, it is not fitting to be concerned with the external appearance of virtues nor to be content with that. I will give you an example.

A person who wants to abandon anger trains himself to quiet his countenance and motions. He avoids having a loud or stern voice and appears to be calm, quiet, and free from any negative emotional reactions. But this calmness is only outward; his heart from within is like a fiery furnace, full of suppressed anger. Assuredly it is good to avoid rage so that you do not sin with your tongue and lose your relationship with others; however, the external calmness of a person is by no means sufficient. There needs to be inner work to calm the heart as well.

Inner calmness is achieved through training the heart on longsuffering, meekness, love, and self-reproach. This fixes your heart, so it does not move toward wrong emotions even if they are not apparent to others. This reminds us of what the Fathers said about the meaning of turning the other cheek.

What is the meaning of, "But whoever slaps you on the right cheek, turn the other to him also" (Matt. 5:39)? Some of the Fathers said, as written in the book of Conferences by John Cassian: "The first slap is from the outside, on the cheek, that is, an external insult. This is met by turning the other cheek which is the inner slap by referring the blame to oneself. You say to yourself," I deserve all this because of my sins."[1] Thus, you take the second slap internally in your heart. Even if we look at the literal, rather than the spiritual, meaning of the verse, the meaning of the commandment is in line with David's behavior when he was insulted by Shimei the son of Gera. When the commander of the army wanted to kill him, David prevented him saying: "So let him curse, because the Lord has said to him, 'Curse David'... maybe that the Lord will look on my affliction" (2 Sam. 16:5-12).

This also conforms with the saying of Saint Abba Antony the Great: "If someone rebukes you, rebuke yourself in turn, as wor-

[1] Conferences 16.22.2

thy of what happened to you." In this way, there will be consistency between your internal and external self, and you will not suffer.

Some people tolerate things outwardly in a seemingly quiet way while they suffer inwardly, feeling injustice. Thus, they experience a conflict between their inner and outer selves. Through inner spiritual work, a person is saved from this contradiction either by humility, by blaming one's self and remembering one's own sins, or by joyfulness, by entering into the fellowship of God's sufferings (Phil. 3:10). Therefore, rejoice in suffering like the Apostles who, after they were beaten, "departed from the presence of the council, rejoicing that they were counted worthy to suffer shame for His name" (Acts 5:41).

Repentance

The outward part of repentance is abandoning sin, staying away from it and from its causes. Nevertheless, a person might leave sin, but in his heart remains desiring it. Can we call this repentance? No, because there needs to be inner work within the heart for a person to reach the point of hating sin. This is true repentance; a person replacing the lusts of the material and the flesh with the desire to live with God.

Here, we would like to explain the true spiritual meaning of a metanoia or prostration. In the metanoia, a person bows down, and his head touches the ground, that is, the dust. This is the outward, apparent work. But inner work should accompany the bowing down of the body; the person should inwardly bow down his soul in contrition, casting off its haughtiness, as David the Prophet said, "My soul clings to the dust" (Psa. 118:25). A brother once said to one of the fathers, "Sometimes I make a metanoia before my brother, but he does not accept it." The father answered, "It is because you did it with a spirit of pride." This means that although the body bowed down, the soul remained prideful and did not cling to the dust.

Repentance, then, whether in reconciling with God or others, is an inner work of convincing the soul of this path of repentance, of its desire to walk it, and of its remorse for its past life. All of these are internal works. The matter is not just abandoning the offenses from the outside because even if we are externally encompassed by obstacles, they cannot harm us so long as the inner heart is victorious. Saint John Chrysostom rightly said, "No one can harm the man who does not harm himself."[2]

Upbringing and Service

Preachers often stand at the pulpit, renouncing the indecent apparel of young women, the long hair of young men, and the like. However, youth may give up all these external matters under certain pressure, while their hearts remain impure. The solution is inner work; bringing the love of God and the love of chastity into the hearts of these people, convincing them that the beauty of the soul is far more important than that of the body. Only then will they abandon their present state willingly and contentedly, replacing it with love and embrace of modesty. This will not be out of obedience or fear for being watched or rebuked, but out of purity of heart. True upbringing, thus, depends on the inner work of convincing and the cultivation of high principles in one's soul.

Therefore, raise your children with care for their inside self before the outer one. Before you use the rod for their outward behavior, cultivate in them the love of God first. Trust that the love of God is much more powerful than any rod and that it can peacefully cast out every sin from the heart. As the Lord Jesus Christ commanded, "first cleanse the inside of the cup and dish, that the outside of them may be clean also" (Matt. 23:26).

The aim of the inner work is first to prevail over the self, and then to attain purity of soul. These aims demand convincing the soul in a sound way, which requires a true understanding of matters. What is the meaning and purpose of life? What is the meaning

---

[2] St. John Chrysostom has an entire work devoted to this subject, which can be found in NPNF, s. 1, v. 9.

of freedom and its boundaries? The meaning of strength, beauty, masculinity? There also needs to be an understanding of the true concept of religion and the proper manner of dealing with people. In instructing people, we do not use the rod, but we use conviction and sound understanding. Afterwards, comes the strengthening of their will, which is the inner work of the heart and mind.

It is very easy to punish and spank, but is this upbringing? No, it is not. Even if it brings about results, in most cases, they are temporary and vanish with external pressures. Does a person who yields to these pressures have any reward from God? What sort of reward when he walks in virtue only externally, and unwillingly? Therefore, inner work has two parts: our work within ourselves and our work within the souls of others.

Prayer and Fasting

Is prayer merely talking with God or does it involve inner work? If so, what type of inner work? Talking with God is the obvious outward act in prayer, but undoubtedly there is a more important inner work. The inner work of prayer is the soul's contact with God, its nearness to Him, and the accompanying feelings of love, reverence, faith, spiritual fervor, and the pleasure of being in His presence.

Prayer sometimes reaches beyond the limits of talking with God, as the spiritual elder said, "Silence your tongue that your heart may speak, and silence your heart that God may speak." This is the inner work of prayer; it is firstly the encounter of man with God. Secondly, it is also listening to the voice of God within the soul, or at least, an intimate spiritual feeling of the Divine presence. Have you reached this level or are you content with the external act? We see, then, that the inner work is partially from you and the other part is granted to you as a gift from God, Himself.

Similarly, many people confine themselves in their fasts to the external act of abstaining from food for a certain period of time and limiting what they eat to unappetizing foods. But the inner work, which is neglected by such people, is that of preventing the soul from any wrong desire in the same manner that the flesh abstains from eating desirous food. A person should use the period of fasting to raise the spirit above the level of the flesh, giving it concentrated spiritual nourishment that lasts even after the period of fasting. Is it so with you? Or do you only give attention to the external, bodily work and think that you fast?

Reading

Although reading is an outward act, meditating on what you read is an inner act. That is why meditation is more important than reading. Understanding is an inner work, and so is the effect of the words on you and the application of what you read. Therefore, the inner work of reading refers to the spiritual work and not merely the filling of your mind with facts and knowledge. The inner work in reading is the transformation of facts and information into life.

Silence

Abstaining from speech is the external act of silence, but silence is not confined to this negative aspect, it has its positive aspects as well. The inner work of silence is delving into one's inner self to gain spiritual benefits, meditate, think on the Divine attributes, and pray. In this manner, a person benefits spiritually from silence. He does not talk with people because he is talking with God. That is why he sits alone—to enjoy God.

However, solitude is not just sitting by oneself. For, what is virtuous about a person sitting alone? A person may sit, yet his thoughts wander here and there. Sitting alone is just an external act, the aim of which is to sit with God or to be alone with Him and enjoy His Divine communion in prayer, meditation, praise, confession, and love. This is the inner act of solitude.

We ought to give attention to the inner work with all our might because the Holy Bible says that "the Kingdom of God is within you" (Luke 17:21). If we attain the Kingdom of God within us through inner work, then we will have reached the depth of the spiritual work, where God reigns over the heart, mind, and all senses and emotions. Every practice of worship that does not bring us to this aim must have strayed from the path.

Inner work has two components: work with God and work with the soul. You work with your soul to control it well, observe its thoughts, feelings and desires, reprove it when it deviates, and restore it to the correct path. Convince your soul about the beauty of the way of the Lord and remind it about eternal life so that it diligently prepares and eagerly strives to attain it. Your work with God is to converse with Him, with affection and love, and to wrestle with Him so that He confirms His Kingdom in your heart.

Having a relationship with God and deepening it day by day is undoubtedly an inner act, which is incompatible with mere external appearances. Therefore, the spiritual life does not merely consist of external practices and laws and statutes, but it is love for God and others. Love is an inner work that demands vigilance, preservation, and growth. Such love relates to those who live in the world. For monks, however, their inner work is higher and deeper. This leads us to ask: What is the meaning of a working monk?

A working monk is one who is continually preoccupied with inner work so that his mind and thoughts are unceasingly engaged with God. If monasticism is said to be the detachment from all to be attached to the One, then, the inner work of the monk is the attachment of his mind unceasingly to God, binding his emotions with His love, and repelling all other thoughts. That is why he must engage himself in prayer, meditation, praise, and spiritual reading so that his mind can always be with God. If he does not do this, his mind will wander and fall into frivolity.

A monk's inner work with God compels him by necessity to keep silent, as Saint Arsenius said, "I cannot speak with both God and men at the same time." Another Father said, "The talkative monk reveals that he is void within," that is, void of the inner work. For this reason, the fathers took refuge in solitude, careful to keep their silence and guard their senses. They continued their inner work with God until they attained unceasing prayer and crucified the mind, preventing it from wandering.

❃ Communion with God ❃

The foremost benefit of inner work is communion with God. The more a person clings to God, the humbler he becomes as he feels his weakness in his inability to detach himself from all to be attached to the One.

However, the devil does not leave this inner work without attacks or warfare. He tries with all his might to disperse a person's thoughts, presenting him tens of subjects and giving him a sense of urgency so as to preoccupy him with them. He may send the person visitors or friends to stop him from his spiritual work. He may even attack a minister with the preoccupations of those in his flock to steal his time and attention away from being alone with God.

CHAPTER 11

Faithfulness

❦ The Importance of Faithfulness and its Bounds ❦

By faithfulness, I do not merely mean honesty in monetary and material matters, such that a person does not rob or plunder others, but I mean faithfulness in its full sense. That is, faithfulness of the whole self in one's behavior and spiritual life: faithfulness in man's relationship with God, others, and himself.

The Lord Jesus Christ called us to this faithfulness when He talked about faithfulness in service and the "faithful and wise steward, whom his master will make ruler over his household, to give them their portion of food in due season" (Luke 12:42). Moreover, the Lord Jesus Christ also mentioned faithfulness as a criterion of judgment and the gateway to enter the Kingdom. For He will say to the person who is worthy of entering into His kingdom, "Well done, good and faithful servant; you were faithful over a few things, I will make you ruler over many things. Enter into the joy of your Lord" (Matt. 25:21,23).

But to what extent should we be faithful? The Lord says, "Be faithful until death, and I will give you the crown of life" (Rev. 2:10). "Until death", that is, to the point at which you sacrifice yourself and your life for the sake of faithfulness. This reminds us of the words of Saint Paul the Apostle to the Hebrews when he rebuked them for their faithlessness in resisting sin, saying, "You have not yet resisted to bloodshed, striving against sin" (Heb. 12:4). "Until death", that is, even if the matter leads to shedding one's blood in striving against sin. In this way, the person is faithful in his relationship with God, not betraying Him by yielding to sin.

Faithfulness helped the righteous attain their goal. Many started the path together, but some attained, others did not, and yet others tarried. What was the reason for this difference? It was because some (but not all) were faithful in their spiritual practices and thus were able to gain crowns.

Faithfulness should be in worldly matters as well as in spiritual matters. Just as the person is concerned about his spiritual life, he should also be faithful in every work he does. The student should be faithful in his studies, striving to perfect his work, pass his exams, achieve the highest grades, be mindful of his time, and keep his appointments. In like manner, an employee or any other person should also be faithful in all their responsibilities.

Joseph the Righteous was a spiritual person who was honest in his work. He was so honest in his service to Potiphar that his work prospered. He was so sincere in his work as a minister for Egypt that he saved it and the surrounding countries from famine. He was so honest even when he was a prisoner that the jailer entrusted him with responsibilities.

Many situations in life test a person's honesty. An example is when a person forges a medical note to claim an unjustified leave from work. It does not suffice him to be dishonest himself, but he makes the doctor sin as well. Another example is when a person claims overtime or reimbursements when he could have performed the work during normal working hours. There are numerous examples, among them are those who spread false news, those who disclose secrets entrusted to them and those who do not perform the task assigned to them in a proper manner.

❖ Faithfulness to God ❖

If God is so faithful to us to the extent of the Incarnation and Redemption, and if His love and His sacrifice have reached such an extent, how much more should we be faithful?

Your faithfulness towards God means that you do not betray

Him at all—like a wife who is faithful to her husband. No matter how much freedom and trust he gives her, she is faithful to him and does not betray him nor has relations with another. Likewise, your soul, which is the bride of Christ, should not betray Him with worldliness, Satan, any lust or evil thought.

Your heart, which belongs to God, should not be bare to His enemies. The faithful person should not be lenient towards any sin because sin is enmity with God. He should not entertain any sinful thought but should immediately cast it out. He should never accept any matter that would sever his unity with God, considering that every sin is foremost directed against God because it is against His love and incompatible with His will. It is against His commandments and against abiding in Him. He should emulate Joseph the Righteous, saying, "How then can I do this great wickedness, and sin against God?" (Gen. 39:9). Joseph considered that sin was not chiefly directed against Potiphar or his wife, but against God. For the same reason, David the Prophet said to the Lord in Psalm 50, "Against You, You only, have I sinned and done this evil in Your sight" (Psa. 50:4).

Sin is separation from, and rebellion against, God. The faithful person in his relationship with God never accepts anything that would separate him from God. As Saint Paul the Apostle said, "For I am persuaded that neither death nor life, nor angels nor principalities nor powers, nor things present nor things to come, nor height nor depth, nor any other created thing, shall be able to separate us from the love of God which is in Christ Jesus our Lord" (Rom. 8:38,39).

Those who truly came to know God never abandoned Him. The penitent saints are examples of this. When they repented and tasted the love of God, they did not return to the sins which would have separated them from it. Rather, they continued to grow in their love for Him until they reached high levels of perfection. Some of these are Saint Augustine, Saint Moses the Black, Saint Mary of Egypt and Saint Pelagia. About his previous life of sin, Saint Augustine said to God, "Late have I loved you, beauty so old and so new: late have I loved you."[1] He acknowledges and considers that while living in sin, he was alienated from the love of God. This is the negative aspect.

The positive aspect of faithfulness to God necessitates that a person be faithful in all his spiritual practices: in his prayers because they are conversing with God, in his reading of the Holy Bible through which he listens to the voice of God, in his contemplation, praise, confessions, partaking of Holy Communion, and in his fasts.

He also should be faithful in his service and spiritual activities. He should be faithful in teaching. As the Apostle said, "But as for you, speak the things which are proper for sound doctrine" (Titus 2:1). He should not present his own opinions as dogmas and should not present to people anything other than the teachings which he received from the Church through Her saints. Saint Paul said to his disciple Timothy, "And the things that you have heard from me, among many witnesses, commit these to faithful men who will be able to teach others also" (2 Tim. 2:2). He should also be faithful in visitations and in bringing back those who have gone astray. The Lord Jesus gave us examples of this in His searching after the lost sheep (Luke 15), in His work for the sake of Zacchaeus and the Sinful Woman, and in saying that He came "to serve and to give His life a ransom for many" (Mark 10:45).

With regard to faithfulness in the service, we quote the words of the Holy Bible, "Cursed is he who does the work of the Lord negligently" (Jer. 48:10). He who is faithful in the work of the Lord acts with complete fervor, all diligence, extreme sincerity, holy zeal, and sincere love. He toils for the sake of the Lord. He does not give sleep to his eyes nor slumber to his eyelids until he finds a place for the Lord in every heart. As is written in the Didascalia the bishop should care for the salvation of all.[2] These

---

[1] St. Augustine, Confessions, Ch. 27.
[2] "For it behoves you, O bishop, as a faithful steward to care for all; for as you bear the sins of all those under your charge, so you should beyond all men receive more abundant glory of God. For you are an imitator of Christ: and as He took upon Him the sins of us all [cf. 1 Pt 2:24], so it

words also apply to all the bishops' assistants.

Such was the faithfulness in the service which our fathers the Apostles lived. They witnessed to the Lord with all sincerity. They were faithful witnesses, spreading the message to all the countries of the world as the Psalm says of them, "Their line has gone out through all the earth, and their words to the end of the world" (Psa. 18). They did their work boldly with all their might, enduring imprisonment, scourging, persecution and torture, saying their famous declaration, "We ought to obey God rather than men" (Acts 5:29). As an example of this faithfulness Saint Paul the Apostle said, "I have fought the good fight, I have finished the race, I have kept the faith" (2 Tim. 4:7), "And I thank Christ Jesus our Lord who has enabled me, because He counted me faithful, putting me into the ministry" (1 Tim. 1:12). That is why Saint Paul praised those who helped him for their faithfulness in the ministry, saying: "Tychicus, a beloved brother and faithful minister in the Lord" (Eph. 6:21), "Epaphras, our dear fellow servant, who is a faithful minister of Christ" (Col. 1:7), "Onesimus, a faithful and beloved brother" (Col. 4:9), and "Timothy, who is my beloved and faithful son in the Lord" (1 Cor. 4:17).

Whether someone is responsible for the service of the Church, a specific part of it, or for a family, in all these cases a service has been entrusted to him to which he must be faithful. For this reason, it is said about the minister that he is entrusted with the ministry; that God entrusted him with the ministry. To this effect, Saint Paul the Apostle says, "preaching which was committed to me," (Titus 1:3) "the gospel for the uncircumcised had been committed to me," (Gal. 2:7) and: "I have been entrusted with a stewardship... woe is me if I do not preach the Gospel" (1 Cor. 9:17,16). Therefore, the service is a commitment before God in which the servant should be faithful for it is not a mere title.

He who is faithful in his relationship with God is also faithful in his promises and vows. From the first vow that his mother uttered to renounce the Satan on his behalf on the day of his

---

behoves you also to bear the sins of all those under your charge..." (Didascalia, ch. 8)

baptism to all the promises which he is or is not readily conscious of, including the promises he makes every time he partakes of the Holy Communion, and his vows on all occasions especially in times of affliction. The Holy Bible says, "It is better not to vow than to vow and not pay" (Ecc. 5:5). That is why you have to sit alone with yourself and recall all of your promises and vows in order to pay them. It is even better to pay them late, than to be completely negligent about them. After committing to a vow or promise do not try to return and discuss the matter anew, negotiate and try to change, replace, or get rid of your vow or promise. Before vowing or promising, the Holy Bible warns you, saying, "Do not be rash with your mouth, and let not your heart utter anything hastily before God" (Ecc. 5:2).

Your faithfulness to God also comprises your honesty in paying tithes and first fruits. They are not yours, but instead they are God's portion. You pay them to those who ought to have them - the church or the poor—otherwise this money would be 'unlawful' to you. You would have kept it with you and been unjust to those who ought to have it. About this, the Holy Bible says, "make friends for yourselves by unrighteous mammon" (Luke 16:9). Thus, says the Lord God in the Book of Malachi the Prophet, "Will a man rob God? Yet you have robbed Me. But you say, 'In what way have we robbed You?' In tithes and offerings" (Malachi 3:8).

❈ Faithfulness to Yourself ❈

This constitutes many elements: your faithfulness over your eternity, your concern about your spirit and spiritual growth, your sincerity in resisting sin and your honesty with your time and intellect.

He who is faithful over his eternity exerts every effort to attain it. He considers himself a sojourner on earth, desiring after nothing in it. All his desires are focused on eternity as the Holy Bible says, "we do not look at the things which are seen, but at the things which are not seen. For the things which are seen are temporary, but the things which are hot seen are eternal" (2 Cor. 4:18).

Therefore, such a person pays more attention to his spirit than to his body, contrary to what we notice in our everyday life. Many care for their body, their food, clothing, health, strength and treatment. However, they may not care at all for their souls as though the thought of their eternity had never crossed their minds!

Those who are faithful over their eternity care for their spiritual nourishment. They provide their spirit with all its needs: the word of God, contemplation, prayer, spiritual songs, spiritual gatherings, and spiritual friendships. They provide it with the nourishment of the Eucharist, the love of God, the fruit of the Spirit and beneficial spiritual practices. Is this the case with you?

Those who are faithful over their eternity give attention to treating their spirit. If they see any spiritual illness creeping into them, they go to the Physician of our bodies and souls, our God Who gives strength through His Holy Spirit. They also consult their spiritual fathers and guides, seeking healing for their souls from every sinful desire and evil thought.

Those who are faithful over their spirit always give attention to their spiritual growth. They are never satisfied with any spiritual level they attain because God asks them to be perfect and to be holy, saying, "Therefore you shall be perfect, just as your Father in heaven is perfect" (Matt. 5:48). Also the Holy Bible says, "but as He who called you is holy, you also be holy in all your conduct" (1 Peter 1:15).

That is why those who are faithful over their spirits constantly hunger and thirst for righteousness. They gain the blessedness of which the Lord promised in the Gospel of Saint Matthew (Matt. 5:6). Their thirst for the Lord does not end. The more they drink the more they ask, saying with David the Prophet, the Psalmist and man of prayer, "My soul thirsts for You; My flesh

longs for You in a dry and thirsty land where there is no water. As the deer pants for the water brooks, so pants my soul for You, O God" (Ps. 62:1; 41:1). No matter how high of a level they attain in virtue, they still feel that they need more, like Saint Paul the Apostle who, although he was caught up to the third heaven (2 Cor. 12:2,4), said, "Not that I have already attained, or am already perfected; but I press on, that I may lay hold of that for which Christ Jesus has also laid hold of me. I do not count myself to have apprehended; but one thing I do, forgetting those things which are behind and reaching forward to those things which are ahead. I press towards the goal for
the prize of the upward call of God in Christ Jesus" (Phil. 3:12-14).

Thus, he who is faithful in his spirituality constantly grows, like a tree that grows and develops daily, whether or not he is aware of this growth. As it is written in the Psalms, "The righteous shall flourish like a palm tree, He shall grow like a cedar in Lebanon" (Psa. 91:12). His prayers are long and deep. He advances in his faith, humility and love. He also advances in giving and sacrifice. He does not stop at a certain point but blames himself whenever he ceases to grow.

In his growth, he does not only seek his eternity, but also his place there. As long as everyone will receive his reward according to his labor (1 Cor. 3:8), so he toils with all his might to receive a greater reward. As "one star differs from another star in glory" (1 Cor. 15:41), so he labors to attain all the heavenly glory, striving in his love for God and growing in this love continually so that he can enjoy these promises in eternity. He feels that his growth in his love for God, not only helps him to attain a more joyous eternal life, but it also protects him from falling. Faithfulness calls him to advance.

Is this so with you? Do you grow every day? Are you standing still and has your growth ceased? Have you gone backwards and your former love has grown cold? Do you still need to repent in order to rise? Ask yourself. If this is so with you, then faithfulness necessitates your vigorous striving to resist sin.

Be vigilant and do not leave any of the doors of your soul open to sin. With all faithfulness, close all the openings through which Satan can enter. Be faithful in controlling your thoughts and senses because the senses are the doors to your thoughts, and your thoughts are a door through which lust enters into the heart. Sing with David the Prophet and say, "Praise the Lord, O Jerusalem! Praise your God, O Zion! For He has strengthened the bars of your gates; and has blessed your children within you" (Psa. 146:12). How true is what is said in the Song of Songs, "A garden enclosed is my sister, my spouse, a spring shut up, a fountain sealed" (Song 4:12). It is a garden full of the fruits of the Holy Spirit, but it is shut before the enemy and all his thoughts and all his wiles. He cannot enter because the Lord is within. It is a temple of His Holy Spirit (1 Cor. 3:16). Therefore, it is firmly shielded against the attacks of the enemy.

Such a faithful soul is like a ship without any holes through which water can enter. It is surrounded with water on all sides, yet only from the outside. The water cannot find an opening through which it can enter. Such is the faithful person. If he finds the devil trying to drill holes for himself in his soul, he hastens without delay to cure it and his soul remains sound. The devil battles against his soul from the outside but is unable to enter.

He who is faithful in his spirituality does not justify himself if he falls. He does not give any excuse for his weakness or the severity of the warfare that encountered him, but he resists unto death. Joseph the Righteous refused to sin, giving not the excuse of his pressing circumstances. Similarly, Daniel the Prophet and the Three Holy Youth cleaved to the Lord, presenting not the excuse of their being prisoners in exile and threats of the lions' den and fiery furnace, were severe and fearful, but they persevered and remained steadfast. Such were the martyrs before their various tortures and terrors. The faithful person is steadfast, fighting the Lord's battle valiantly. He does not claim that anything happened against his will. He withstands the toughest spiritual battle as

David did before Goliath the giant. With all faith and courage he fights, trusting that God will grant him victory.

He who is faithful in his warfare is mindful of what is said of the valiant soldier, that he fights with the last bullet and to the last man. In other words, he fights with all his effort and with all the help and grace he is given. He does not yield at all to the enemy, nor betray the Lord, nor depend on presenting excuses. The Holy Bible and history of the Church are full of examples of valiant and faithful individuals who persisted in the love of God despite their challenging circumstances.

If there is faithfulness of heart, there will be faithfulness of will. He who has the will is capable. If he lacks strength, he will ask for it from above and it will be granted to him. That is why in Saint Peter the Apostle's epistle after explaining that the devil roars like a lion, seeking whom he may devour, later says, "Resist him, steadfast in the faith" (1 Peter 5:9). Yes, resistance denotes faithfulness, provided that it is a serious resistance from the depths of the heart and constitutes the whole of one's will.

What will the result of resistance be? Saint James the Apostle says, "Resist the devil and he will flee from you" (James 4:7). Therefore, the importance lies in the pure and faithful heart which wills to resist and prompts the will to resist. That is why the Lord, before healing the paralyzed man at Bethesda, inquired about the state of the man's heart, asking him, "Do you want to be made well?"

One of the devil's practices is that he takes your pulse first. Would you give way to him even in the very smallest matter? If you would, he dares to move to a greater matter. If you open before him a little hole, even the size of the eye of a needle, he will attack you more violently. For there and then he realizes that your faithfulness to God is imperfect. If you give way in the small matters, he is encouraged to find in you a place for himself or a vulnerable point to use. If you are lax in controlling the senses, he will attack your thoughts. If you are careless in controlling your thoughts, he will fight you with lust. And if you are negligent in lust, he will fight you to put it into action. Therefore, do not be lax in anything at all. If you fall in one step, rise quickly. Do not advance to another step. Faithfulness necessitates that you watch over your soul and not be negligent in preserving its purity and salvation. If you find the devil throwing something evil into your thoughts quickly remember the words of the Holy Bible, "Bringing every thought into captivity to the obedience of Christ" (2 Cor. 10:5).

He who is faithful over his eternity and spirituality is watchful over his soul. He does not wait until he has a deadly fall, but if he finds apathy creeping into his soul he hastens to cure it before it develops. He resists sin at its onset and does not wait until it reaches a serious level that would afflict him. This is because if he slacks in resisting the devil, the devil will not be slack with him.

He who is faithful does not use the weakness of his abilities as an excuse, but he tries to continually develop them. He also does not present his incapability as an excuse because God is capable of granting him strength. God is faithful who does not permit anyone to be tempted beyond his capability. Thus, says the Apostle, "But God is faithful, who will not allow you to be tempted beyond what you are able, but with the temptation will also make the way of escape, that you may be able to bear it" (1 Cor. 10:13).

The spiritual person is honest regarding time. He uses it in whatever it is beneficial to him in every respect: spiritually, intellectually and in serving others. He sees that time is part of his life, a gift entrusted to him, which he should not waste but spend in doing good. Therefore, look how much of your time you have wasted in vain and ask yourself, "Am I faithful regarding my time?"

Consider your faithfulness on the Day of the Lord. It is the Lord's Day. It belongs to Him. If you are not faithful in spending this day in a spiritual way, then you are neither faithful to the Lord nor to yourself. Just as Sunday is the Day of the Lord so also are the feasts of the Lord. They belong to Him. They are holy days. The Lord says in the Book of Leviticus, "The feasts of the Lord, which you shall proclaim to be holy convocations, these are My feasts" (Lev. 23:2). The Lord mentioned that His feasts are as holy as the Sabbath (Lev. 23:8,25,32,39). Are you faithful on the day of the Lord and His feasts? Do you keep them holy?

❈ Faithfulness to Others ❈

As much as a faithful person is faithful regarding the Kingdom of God within himself, he is also faithful over the Kingdom of God within others. He loves others as himself. He cares for them as he cares for himself. He is concerned about their salvation, their growth and their happiness as much as he cares for himself. For such is the commandment (Matt. 22:39).

When God created the trees, He did not create them barren, but He put in it an important quality which made it "yield fruit according to its kind, whose seed is in itself" (Gen. 1:11). He also created the herb to yield seed according to its kind. Are you similar to these trees? Do you bring forth fruit of your kind, and does your seed yield fruit of its kind as well? Do you spread the Kingdom of Heaven wherever you go? To what extent are you faithful to the Kingdom of God?

I will ask you some questions. Respond to yourself and also before your father of confession: If you enter a house, does the Word of God enter with you? If you live among people, friends, acquaintances or colleagues, do you bear in them spiritual fruit whether by word or by good example or by both? If you visit people, do they say in their hearts, "Today Christ visited us"? Does the blessing of God reach people through you? Do you become in your faithfulness, salt for the earth and light for the world? Is this not the Lord's commandment in His Sermon on the Mount (Matt. 5:13,14)? Are we faithful in keeping this commandment? Saint Peter the Apostle says, "receiving the end of your faith—the salvation of your souls" (1 Peter 1:9), and Saint Paul the Apostle says, "I have become all things to all men, that I might by all means save some" (1 Cor. 9:22), and moreover he says, "I have made myself a servant to all, that I might win the more" (1 Cor. 9:19). Saint Ignatius of Antioch was surnamed 'Theophorus' which means "God-bearer." Are you also a Theophorus, bearing God to all so that everyone sees Him in your life? Do you build His kingdom in all of your relationships?

❊ Faithful in Little ❊

Someone may ask, "The spiritual path is long. How can I reach its end? How can I attain holiness, without which no one will see God? How can I reach the perfection that is required of me?" The reply is easy and attainable: Be faithful in the few things and God will entrust you with much. For this is God's way and this is His promise. This is what He will say to people in the Day of Judgment (Matt. 25:21, 23). Therefore, this is all that you have to do. You do not have to think about reaching the destination all at once. But you should know that a single step is the beginning of the long journey.

Be faithful in the first step and God will entrust you with the rest. Be faithful in your spiritual goal and God will design for you the means to reach the goal. Be faithful in your intentions and God will entrust you with its fulfillment.

The devil may complicate the way and make it appear difficult before you. He tries to instill fears in you—trying to make you feel burdened by all the demands which seem beyond your power and capabilities to lead you to despair. But God only requires of you faithfulness in the little things. As for the many things, He will entrust them to you. Therefore, it is beautiful that Psalm 118 starts with the verse, "Blessed are the blameless in the way" (Psalm 119:1). It suffices that you walk in the path of the Lord blamelessly. That is what He requires of you. As for reaching the destination, leave it to Him. He manages when and how.

❈ Service and Consecration ❈

Someone may ask, "How can my whole life be for the Lord? Is it possible that God would grant me to devote my life to Him? Is it possible that all my life can be for His service? How?" I say to you: Start with the little you are capable of, by giving your spare time to the Lord. Start by devoting the Lord's Day to Him alone. If you are faithful in this, God may entrust you with much. Be faithful in your service by teaching in Sunday School and other classes of Christian education. Then, if God is pleased with your faithfulness, He will entrust you with a greater service. Be faithful in every service commended to you, then God will entrust you with dedicating your life to Him.

There are some people who think that they cannot serve the church unless they are in a position of authority. One of them may say: "If I was a bishop or a metropolitan, I would do this and that. If I were a priest, I would have corrected this neighborhood, city, or town." He may say these things even though he is not involved in the service or his service is a failure. As for you, do not say such things.

Be faithful in your own house then the Holy Spirit will entrust you with the House of God. Do the little that you can. Be faithful in raising your children, and God will present to you His children to raise. It was most likely for this reason, in mentioning the conditions of anointing the clergy, that the Holy Bible says, "having faithful children not accused of dissipation or insubordination" (Titus 1:6), and that the clergyman should be "one who rules his own house well, having his children in submission with all reverence (for if a man does not know how to rule his own house, how will he take care of the Church of God?)" (1 Tim. 3:4, 5).

Therefore, how can he who is incapable of a few things be capable of many? How can he who cannot rule their own house be entrusted to rule a congregation? Faithfulness is tested primarily in a few things, not only in regard to a house or Sunday School class. For, there is something prior to all these. It is the faithfulness of the servant regarding his own life and how he manages it.

Be faithful over your own soul and God will entrust you with the souls of others. Test your faithfulness first in managing your own soul which is always with you, in which you know all its secrets and weaknesses. You can reprimand it and it will obey you. If you are not faithful in managing your own soul, how then can you be trusted to manage others? If you are not able to lead one soul that is within you, how can you lead many other souls? One of the saints said, "He who is not honest over one denarii is a liar to think that he will be honest over a thousand."

What is important is faithfulness and not the position you occupy. Saint Stephen was not one of the Twelve Apostles, nor was he a bishop of the Church. He was just a deacon. Nevertheless, he was so faithful that many believed through him, the councils of philosophers were brought to shame, and he became chief of the Church leaders. In like manner, was the deacon, Saint Athanasius, the Reader Ephraim the Syrian, and Saint Simon the Cobbler.

Saint Reweis was faithful even though he had no rank. He was not a deacon, reader, monk, member of the clergy, or a church servant. Nevertheless, he was faithful in his spiritual life relationship with God, becoming one of the saints of his generation. He was loved and highly esteemed by the Pope of his generation. Therefore, it is a matter of being faithful in life and not in rank or status. How faithful are you in your responsibilities, regardless of how small they may be?

The protagonist of any story is not necessarily a king, chief, or leader. Rather, he may be a servant, but the protagonist is esteemed and loved by the people because of his honesty in perfecting his role, regardless of what it may be. Therefore, be faithful in the little you have, and know that the servant with two talents received the same blessing from the Lord as the one with five talents because they were equally faithful in the talents they had received. The Lord's blessing of them was centered on their faithfulness rather than the amount of talents (Matt. 25:21,23).

David was faithful in shepherding the flock of sheep, so God entrusted him to shepherd His people. He was faithful in the little which was the few sheep in the wilderness (1 Sam. 17:28). When a lion and a bear attacked one of his sheep, he attacked it and saved the lamb from it. When the Lord saw his faithfulness, He entrusted him to save a whole army from the mighty Goliath. When he was faithful in confronting Goliath, God entrusted him with the whole kingdom.

So, it should be with you. Begin this quest for faithfulness. Be faithful in the house of Potiphar and God will entrust you with the palace of Pharaoh and the land of Egypt. Be faithful in the little resources you have, and God will entrust you with much more. Be faithful in offering the handful of flour which you have and the little oil in the jar as the widow of Zarephath was, then the Lord will entrust you with the bin of flour which shall not be used up, and the jar of oil which will not run dry throughout the time of famine (1 Kings 17:12,16).

❈ The Will and the Mind ❈

You may stand helpless before weaknesses and sins that prevail over you as though they were firmly fixed habits, crying with the Apostle, "but how to perform what is good I do not find. For the good that I will to do, I do not do; but the evil I will not to do, that I practice" (Rom. 7:18,19). What shall I say to you then?

Be faithful in what is within your own will and God will entrust you with what is beyond your will. Be faithful in resisting voluntary sins and God will entrust you with the resistance of involuntary sins. You may ask, "What shall I do about the impure dreams which come to me when I am asleep, which I am unable to rid myself of and have become firmly rooted in my subconscious?"

I say to you: Be faithful in restraining your conscious mind and

God will grant you control of the subconscious. Be faithful in resisting the sins committed while you are awake and God will grant you to resist the sins during sleep. Be faithful in guarding your mind during the day and God will entrust you with purity of mind during your sleep. If you are vigilant over the purity of your thoughts while you are awake, then the time will come when your thoughts will be pure while you are asleep. Let your thoughts be holy during the day and their sanctity will accompany you during the night.

If you are faithful in controlling your senses, God will grant you victory in the warfare of thoughts because the senses are the doors to the mind and the causes of thought. If you are faithful in abandoning the causes of sinful thoughts, God will protect you from these sinful thoughts. If you are faithful in fighting your thoughts, then God will entrust you with purity of heart which is greater. If you are faithful in keeping this purity then God will grant you the crown of righteousness on the Last Day (2 Tim. 4:8), in the place where sin is not known.

❖ Faithfulness in Love ❖

You say, "I want to reach perfect love, to love God with all my heart and with all my might (Deut. 6:5) and to love everyone, even my enemies, and to love what is good. Is it possible for me to attain this virtue which seems so difficult?" I say to you: "Start with the little and you will attain much."

If you are faithful in keeping the virtue of the fear of God, then God will entrust you with the virtue of love. This is because "The fear of the Lord is the beginning of wisdom" (Proverbs 9:10). If you are faithful in the fear of God and keep His commandments, God will entrust you with the love that casts out fear (1 John 4:18). Faithfulness in one level which is conducive to faithfulness in a higher one. You may ask, "How can I keep the commandments when I love the world and there are some commandments that contradict the desires of my heart?" I say to you: Start with self-coercion. Force yourself to do good.

If you are faithful in self-coercion, you will inevitably reach the love of goodness because love for God and goodness are not the starting point, but the result of a long spiritual endeavor. Therefore, force yourself to do good. When you practice it, you will taste of its sweetness. Then, you will love it and do it out of love without having to force yourself. In this way, God will have entrusted you with much.

In like manner, if you are faithful in loving your brother whom you have seen, you will reach the love of God whom you have not seen (1 John 4:20). Therefore, start with this little which is love for people and you will reach much which is love for God. But you may ask, "How can I reach the love of people when they include enemies and opponents? How can I reach the love of enemies?" You reach them through the same rule: that is, by being faithful in the little things.

Be faithful in loving your relatives and you will love your acquaintances. Be faithful in loving your acquaintances, then you will love your enemies. The heart which is used to loving will reach a point where hatred is completely eradicated from it. Then, enmity will only be one-sided. It will be from your enemies and not from you.

❈ Faithfulness in Bodily Virtues and Spiritual Growth ❈

He who is faithful in virtues practiced by the body, is elevated to virtues of the spirit. He who is faithful in making his body fast from food, God will entrust with fasting from sin. He who fasts from idle talk, abstains from evil thoughts, and restrains his heart from lust. But he who is not faithful in abstaining from food—and this is a little task which does not need much effort —how then can he attain to the fasting of the spirit? One of the saints said, "Through stillness of body we acquire stillness of soul." Stillness of the soul is a great thing which we do not reach unless we are faithful in observing stillness of the body. This means that the body should not be engaged in wandering from one place to another, and the senses should be restrained from engaging in unbeneficial things.

In like manner, we acquire reverence of the soul through the reverence of the body. Through faithfulness in humility of the body we acquire humility of the soul. He who prays reverently with his body —while standing, lifting his eyes, controlling his senses and motions, kneeling at the time of kneeling, prostrating at the time of prostration—God will undoubtedly endow with worshipping in spirit and truth. Reverence will certainly spring forth in the heart of the one who faithfully bows down when he says Agios (i.e., Holy).

In this way, we benefit from taking off our shoes when we enter or worship before the Sanctuary. These are physical gestures, but if they are performed with devotion and faith, they transfer to the reverence of the body to the spirit, and the spirit will also worship reverently. This is due to the unity of the body and the spirit.

Thus, if we are faithful with our physical temple, it will become a temple for God. If we are faithful in the physical body, the Lord will entrust us with an illumined spiritual body in the Resurrection (1 Cor. 15:44). If we are faithful in material matters, God will entrust us with spiritual matters. Let us take prayer as an example.

❖ Faithfulness in Prayer ❖

Someone may ask, "To what extent ought men to pray always and not lose heart (Luke 18:1)? And how can we keep the commandment: 'Pray without ceasing' (1 Thess. 5:17) Isn't that too much for us?"

Yes, it is too much if you consider it the starting point. But you start with the little, then God will entrust you with much. Be faithful in getting used to prayer, then God will entrust you with lengthy prayer. If you are faithful in the Lord's Prayer and say it with depth, meaning every word you say, there is no doubt that it will open doors of contemplation and lead you to many other prayers. If you are faithful in the set prayers, God will entrust you with the prayer of the heart.

The remaining problem before us is the issue of time, which is raised by some. We reply that if a person is faithful in prayer during the time available to him, then God will make more time available to him in which he can pray. But the problem is that we have plenty of time in which we can pray, but we waste it and are not faithful in our desire to pray.

Some also raise the question of the levels of prayer, spiritual trances and visions, theoria prayer with tears, and how they can be attained. We reply with the same principle: He who is faithful in the little, God will entrust him with much. Be faithful in praying ardently and with understanding, then God will entrust you with prayer with tears. Be faithful in praying constantly and with love for God, then God will entrust you with other levels of prayer. They will come spontaneously without you desiring them as levels because the subject of levels may entail pride. The spiritual life is a spiritual ladder. You cannot reach the top step unless you pass peacefully through all the preceding ones.

❈ Examples of Faithfulness ❈

Be faithful in what is in your hand and God will entrust you with what is in His hand. Be faithful in using your abilities and God will entrust you with abilities you do not possess. If you perfect walking with the footmen without getting weary, God will entrust you with contending with horses (Jer. 12:5). If you are faithful in fighting visible sins God will entrust you with victory over the hidden sins and lusts. If you are faithful to God in your childhood and adolescence, God will grant you faithfulness in the wars that beset youth. If you are faithful in accepting Leah, God will entrust you to marry Rachel (Gen. 29:27). If you have been faithful in sojourning in the Wilderness of Sinai, God will entrust you with the promised land of Canaan. If you are faithful in this limited and short life, God will entrust you with eternal life.

Thus, it is essential that you be faithful in everything your hand touches no matter how small it may be. So, be faithful in the one talent you have and God will entrust you with five talents. Be faithful in the visible matters and He will entrust you with the invisible matters—those things which no eye has seen, nor ear heard, neither have come upon the heart of man (1 Cor. 2:9). "Be faithful in the fruit of the Spirit and God will entrust you with the gifts of the Spirit. Do not be quick in seeking gifts (1 Cor. 12) without first acquiring the fruit (Gal. 5:22,23) because in the characteristics of the spiritual path, the fruit should precede the gifts of
the Spirit.

If our father, Adam, had been faithful in the little, which was not to eat from one of the trees, he would not have gone through all that happened to him. If he had succeeded in passing the test, he would have been able to eat from the tree of life.

One of the monastic canons is that he who is faithful in the period of coenobitic life and acquiring its virtues can then enter the life of solitude if he wishes. One of the monks said to his spiritual father, "I want to dwell in solitude because I cannot tolerate the trouble of the brethren." The father replied, "If you cannot bear the troubles of the brethren in the coenobitic life, how then, can you tolerate the wars of the devils in solitude?" The penitent thief was faithful during the five hours he spent on the Cross and God granted him to enter with Him into Paradise.

One of the fathers asked his son to clean a field from thorns. When the son went and found the field full of thorns, he was despondent and slept without doing anything. When his father knew what had happened, he said to him, "My son, everyday clean an area only as big as the size of your bed and there will come a time when the whole field will be clear of thorns."

Saint Abraam the Bishop of Fayoum was faithful in the virtue of mercy. He gave whoever asked him and kept nothing for himself but gave it all to the needy. When God saw his great faithfulness, he entrusted him with a larger and greater act of mercy. He endowed him with the gift of healing the sick. Thus, Saint Abraam was faithful in the few things.

CHAPTER 12

Diligence

❈ The Importance of Seriousness ❈

The devil fights diligence for many reasons; it is one of the most important characteristics of the spiritual path without which man cannot attain his goal. If we were to ask: How did the saints reach those high levels in the life of the Spirit, the answer would be because they walked the spiritual path with utter diligence. They had a clear path set before them that they followed with steadfastness, without deviating to the left or to the right. They had immovable principles which they adhered to, never allowing any circumstances to get in their way.

Thus, the saints quickly attained their goal. Abba Mishael the Anchorite was diligent in his monastic path from the very first day, becoming an anchorite at the age of seventeen! His spiritual father, Abba Isaac, witnessed the severe strictness with which he treated himself. Saints Maximous and Domadious had reached high levels of spirituality before the beard of one of them could grow. Their prayers were like beams of light ascending to heaven, and that was because they walked diligently in the spiritual path. Saint Theodore, the disciple of Abba Pachomius, and Saint John the Short became spiritual guides of monastic life in their generations despite being young men.

What caused Saint Abba Antony the Great to become a monk other than diligence? He heard the verse which says, "If you want to be perfect, go, sell what you have and give to the poor, and you will have treasure in heaven; and come, follow Me" (Matt. 19:21). The whole congregation in the Church heard this verse, but Saint Antony was the only one who diligently applied it. He also heard the words: "If you were a monk you would have gone to the mountain in the wilderness because this place is not suitable for monks" and said, "This is God's voice addressing me." So, he rose with diligence and entered the depth of the wilderness, establishing monastic life.

Which one of us has this diligence in carrying out the commandments, meticulously and speedily? These were examples from the lives of monastics. In the field of service, we can take Saint John the Baptist as an example. The length of his service was one year, during which he preached repentance and prepared people for the coming of the Lord. He was so diligent in his service that the Lord said of him, "Among those born of women there has not risen one greater than John the Baptist" (Matt. 11:11). We also mention the diligence of Saint Paul the Apostle who labored more abundantly than all of the Apostles who preceded him (1 Cor. 15:10).

Diligence in life is an indication of courage and a strong personality. He who is serious in his spirituality respects himself, his principles, his word, and the spiritual path he walks in. He is steadfast and unshakeable, like a great ship sailing vigorously in the sea of life towards its goal, and not like a boat that is hit and tossed about by the waves in every direction.

It is surprising that some people are diligent in their material and worldly affairs, but not in their spiritual life. They work diligently to earn money, get a promotion, maintain their position, or avoid punishment. As for their spirituality, they lack the inner motivation that pushes them to diligence, most likely because the fear of God is not in their hearts and eternity is not before their eyes. Such people are not committed to a clear spiritual path.

❈ The Qualities of a Diligent Person ❈

He who is not diligent in his spirituality fluctuates between highs and lows. Erratic, he falls and rises; rises and falls. Sometimes he is fervent in Spirit and at other times he is lukewarm or utterly distant from his spiritual life. Sometimes he prays and at other times neglects his prayers. He may or may not read the Holy Bible. If he finds time he sits with God, and if he does not, he is not bothered and is completely apathetic. His life and worship are characterized by idleness. About such people the Holy Bible says, "Cursed is he who does the work of the Lord negligently" (Jer. 48:10).

Seriousness in the spiritual life does not tolerate negligence, idleness, hesitation, or relapse. Nor does it permit faltering between the love of the world and the love of God. He who is serious is never indifferent towards God. He walks in God's commandments decisively, meticulously, and profoundly with an obedience free from controversy or negotiation. Our father Abraham walked in the commandment of obedience with utter diligence, taking his only son to offer him as a burnt offering to the Lord. He did not argue with God, nor did he object to His command. Rather, he obeyed with a heart steadfast and unwavering towards God. Such is the constancy of obedience.

In like manner was Joseph the Righteous. He diligently obeyed the commandments and preserved his chastity even though it led to his imprisonment. Daniel the Prophet was diligent in his worship to the Lord even though it led to him being thrown into the lions' den. He who is diligent has a strong heart that does not weaken in the face of external circumstances. John the Baptist was diligent in keeping the Lord's commandments, saying to King Herod, "It is not lawful for you to have your brother's wife" (Mark 6:18), even though this led to his imprisonment and martyrdom.

He who is diligent does not excuse himself or justify his sins; he maintains his courage irrespective of external circumstances. The chaste Joseph was constrained by circumstances, he was a slave under the authority of a master and his master's wife was capable of harming him, yet he did not succumb or yield to sin. Daniel the Prophet did not permit himself to eat from the king's delicacies although he was a captive, governed by rules of captivity. He was ardent in his convictions, irrespective of the circumstances.

Moreover, the spiritual person is also diligent in his repentance. He is serious in abandoning sin and does not return to it. He is diligent in resisting sin, unlike the Hebrews whom Saint Paul rebuked, saying, "You have not yet resisted to bloodshed, striving against sin" (Heb. 12:4). How deep is this phrase "to bloodshed"...! He who is diligent in his repentance does not postpone his repentance, like Felix the governor (Acts 24:25) and Agrippa (Acts 26:28). Instead, he is like the Prodigal Son who rose immediately and went to his father, repenting with a contrite heart. Diligence in repentance is highlighted in the words of the spiritual father who said, "I do not recall the devils causing me to fall into the same sin twice." This is because he recognized his sin and did not return to it again. But he who, after confessing and partaking of the Holy Communion, repeats the same sins and gives the same confession, is by no means serious in his repentance.

In the famous stories of repentance of saints such as Mary of Egypt, Pelagia and Moses the Black, we notice something important: repentance was a turning point in their life without return to sin. It was a serious repentance. They moved from sin to purity, advanced to holiness, and then attained perfection. They were transformed from sinners into saints, becoming examples of the life of righteousness, a blessing for others, and even spiritual guides. More importantly, they were serious in denouncing Satan and all his evil works. They were serious in their reconciliation with God and in their desire to live a life of virtue. But those who fall into sins everyday, depending on the words of the Psalm, "He has not dealt with us according to our sins, nor punished us according to our iniquities" (Psa. 102:10), have not truly repented, and God's mercy is for those who are serious in their repentance.

He who is diligent in his spiritual path is characterized by continuous growth. Diligence gives him spiritual fervor which motivates him to advance and strive for the sake of purity and perfection to the farthest extent. With diligence and persistence, he gives God all his might, the entirety of his resources, the extent of his will, and the whole of his heart. He acts with the grace granted to him, exerts all his efforts without complacency, and draws closer to God each day. He advances in the depth of Divine love, and in comprehending and practicing virtues. He does not give in to his ego, gratify it, or excuse it for any shortcomings. If he grows slack, he forces himself to do God's work so that he may turn it into a habit and perform it with love.

He who is diligent is not mindful of his personal desires but sacrifices every pleasure for the sake of the Lord. Such were those who were trained in diligence; they labored for the sake of the Lord, sacrificing their comfort for the sake of their spiritual life. For example, Saint Paul of Tammouh exerted himself in his asceticism, striving, and subjecting his body to his spirit so much that the Lord said to him, "Enough toil, My beloved Paul!" In like manner was David the Prophet who said, "Surely I will not go into the chamber of my house, or go up to the comfort of my bed; I will not give sleep to my eyes or slumber to my eyelids, until I find a place for the Lord and a dwelling place for the Mighty God of Jacob" (Psa. 131:3-5). Such is diligence in the spiritual life.

He who is diligent does not turn the hardships he encounters into excuses. He surmounts them and refuses to yield, struggling and praying, pursuing the ideals, and placing before him the words of the Apostle, "Run in such a way that you may obtain it" (1 Cor. 9:24). Thus, he is always fervent in the Spirit (Rom. 12:11). So long as the ideals are set before him, he is not satisfied with half-solutions nor with passing just one stage of the path, but he continues diligently pressing on towards perfection. Thus, he is constantly in ascent towards God.

Naturally, he who advances unceasingly does not relapse or revert because he takes everything seriously. He is diligent in his life of repentance and does not entertain evil thoughts. He is serious in his spiritual walk and in practicing virtue. He does not abandon his spiritual exercises whatever the reason may be. He is serious in every vow he makes before God and does not try to change his mind, either by negotiating, postponing or exchanging. However, he attends to perform it with all diligence and speed, placing before him the words of the Holy Bible, "It is better not to vow than to vow and not pay" (Ecc. 5:5). Jephthah the Gileadite is an example of the seriousness of vows (Judges 11:30-39).

He who is serious in worship is not satisfied with its outward acts, for he is more concerned with the essence and depth of the spiritual endeavor. That is why he is profound in his worship, ensuring that it is in faith with humility and fervor, a contrite heart, understanding, concentration, and heartfelt love for God. He does not allow his mind to wander here or there, nor does he allow his senses to roam, but he pours himself out in prayer and contemplation, doing prostrations and fasting.

He does not permit his mind to wander outside the church when his body is inside. He is also diligent in his service, performing every responsibility entrusted to him successfully and with perfection, whether it be in the church, his job, or other projects.

❀ Satan's Temptations ❀

Satan fights diligence with every possible means, using even scriptural references. He may call it literalism, or submission to the law instead of grace. However, grace is not an excuse for laziness, indolence, or apathy. When Satan argues that diligence is against flexibility we reply by saying flexibility is not a domain for apathy, carelessness, and lack of commitment. When he claims that diligence is against the glorious liberty of the children of God (Rom. 8:21), we respond by saying Freedom is not freedom if it conflicts with a commandment. For, true freedom is freedom from sin. Therefore, we believe that diligence is connected with faithfulness, precision, and commitment.

CHAPTER 13

Precision

In order to understand meticulousness at its depth let us presume the following. Suppose an angel declares to a person that his life on earth will end after a week. Undoubtedly, during that week, the person will walk with every possible precision in order to prepare himself for his eternal life. It is on this criterion that we would like to measure the life of precision.

❊ The Importance of Precision ❊

Precision is one of the characteristics of the spiritual path. The spiritual person is precise in everything: his relationship with God, with people, and with himself. He is precise in every behavior, word, and thought. He is precise in his senses, feelings, intentions, appointments, time, and even regulations that govern him.

He who is precise is not only meticulous when he is among people but even more so when he is alone in his private room. Precision is relatively easy in the presence of people because by nature we do not like to be criticized by others and fear exposing our faults and weaknesses before them. That is why the true criterion of our precision is made manifest when we are alone, seen by no one. If we are precise when we are alone, then it is a true precision without hypocrisy.

The precision of a spiritual person is a spontaneous part of his nature and not just an attempt or practice. His precision is driven by internal motivation as it constitutes part of his principles and values. Even if he is not seen by people, he likes to be blameless before God who sees him, as well as before the angels and the souls of the saints. Are you precise within yourself irrespective of people's judgments?

But, what is precision? Precision is taking heed so as not to make the slightest error. It is sound and careful behavior in the pursuit of the highest possible level of perfection, without indifference, apathy, or negligence. Precision is thus a step towards perfection. He who is precise and careful not to fall into small errors will find it difficult to fall into great ones. He who takes heed with all his might not to fall into sins of thoughts will not easily fall into sins of deeds.

❊ Precision and Meticulousness ❊

Let everyone take heed to differentiate between precision and scrupulosity. Scrupulosity is seeing errors where there are none or enlarging the assessment of an error, it is the unreasonable feeling of guilt or the excess love of meticulousness to the point of straying away from the truth and condemning righteous behavior.

Scrupulosity is a type of Pharisaism and literalism. It is superficial and void of understanding. It is what the Scribes and Pharisees used in consecrating the Sabbath. This was not precision, but literalism lacking spirit or depth and leading to misunderstanding the commandment. We refuse to call this precision. For precision is sound spiritual behavior that takes the middle position between apathy and scrupulosity.

Precision can be likened to the scale of a chemist. Every component in a medicine has its precise weight which, if increased or decreased, could cause harm. Similar is a precise spiritual life. He who is precise watches his soul, examines it, and does not allow it to become lenient. He observes his principles and values and does not descend below their standards because they constitute explicit characteristics of his spiritual path.

❊ Areas of Precision ❊

He who is precise is careful with his time, seeing that it is part of his life, he does not spend one minute of it on wasteful or useless matters. He arranges his time, balancing it to take care of all his responsibilities.

Just as he is precise with his own time, he is also cognizant about the time of others. A man whose time is not valuable in his eyes does not value other people's time. You often see him wasting another person's time with his visits, problems, or talks while the other is too embarrassed to take leave of him. The precise person, however, respects his life and time as much as those of others. He does not allow himself to waste his time in trivial matters nor does he give conversations or visits more time than is necessary.

He is also careful to give his spirituality its due time. He is precise over the time which he sets apart for his prayers, contemplations, spiritual readings, church services, services, and spiritual gatherings. He is precise over the Day of the Lord and his spiritual life, ensuring they do not get lost amidst the tumults of the various distractions. He remains precise in his prayers, careful that they should be with understanding and fervor, contrition, depth, faith, love, and humility. In his prayers, he neither prays too quickly that the prayers lose their depth, nor does he allow his mind to wander and become distracted. He neglects neither the prayers of the hours nor the psalms.

Moreover, he worships God precisely. If he makes the Sign of the Cross, he does it accurately keeping in mind its spiritual and dogmatic meaning. He does so reverently, with faith in its spiritual effect and power. For him, the Sign of the Cross is not a mere hasty motion without understanding or reverence.

Upon entering the church, he is precise in his prayers and movements, restraining his eyes from wandering around. He does not talk with anyone inside the church and does not engage in anything other than worship. He does not walk too hastily but enters the church quietly so as not to lose the reverence of the place, singing the Psalm, "But as for me, I will come into Your house in the multitude of Your mercy; in fear of You I will worship toward Your holy temple" (Psa. 5:7). He prostrates himself, then stands in his place with all reverence, careful in what he does, guarding his mind, senses, and heart so that when the priest says, "Lift up your hearts," he responds truthfully, saying, "We have them with the Lord."

Furthermore, a spiritual person is precise in his thoughts and does not wait to expel any erroneous ideas. He is always careful to keep away idle and vain thoughts in order to keep his mind pure before God. He puts before him the words of the Apostle, "bringing every thought into captivity to the obedience of Christ" (2 Cor. 10:5). But he who entertains any thought is not precise in controlling them.

The spiritual person is precise even in his speech. He examines every word before uttering it, with regard to its meaning and suitability to the occasion and the audience. He who talks and regrets what he says is not precise, neither is he who is blamed for his words yet claims he "did not mean it." He who hurts the feelings of others is also not precise in his speech. Hastiness is one of the causes for this lack of precision. Being hasty to give an opinion, to judge others, or to lose one's temper makes a person more likely to err and to lose precision in his speech.

But he who is slow to speak and examines every word before saying it is precise. That is why the Apostle says, "Therefore, my beloved brethren, let every man be swift to hear, slow to speak, slow to wrath" (James 1:19). For in slowness and discretion, man can control what he wants to say by selecting the suitable words. He who is slow is more accurate in his speech because he realizes that he cannot change or withdraw his words after uttering them, they already count against him!

As a person ought to be precise in his speech, he also ought to be precise in his jokes and laughter. Laughter should not turn into a type of sarcasm or ridicule, using certain people as a subject of humor or mockery to amuse others, but hurting their feelings in the process. Everyone has the right to laugh with others but not to laugh at them. Therefore, a spiritual person should be precise in his jokes and laughter so that he may not offend or degrade anybody, even in an unintentional or joking manner. He should not joke as he likes without taking heed of his effect on his listeners.

The spiritual person should also be precise in his criticism, blame, and admonishing of others. He should not offend anyone while advising them, nor bring anyone down while rebuking them. Our Lord Jesus Christ warned us, saying, "And whoever says to his brother, 'Raca' shall be in danger of the council. But whoever says, 'You fool!' shall be in danger of hell fire" (Matt. 5:22). The word 'Raca' is the smallest word of disrespect! How often do people use the word 'fool' and its various derivatives, undermining the intelligence and understanding of others? As for the precise person, he should not do so. Notice how the Lord Jesus used the most decent words in his discourse with the Samaritan Woman, leading her to repentance without offending her at all. If He had used what people call frankness to confront the erring person, she would have been offended and He would not have won her soul.

Precision appears in the responsibilities entrusted to a person whether it be spiritual, financial, or social. His meticulousness leads him to success and perfection, winning people's respect and trust. He does not try to give excuses and justify himself in the case of any shortcomings as he considers self-justification against precision. There are many who are precise in accusing others but do not use the same measure when accusing themselves. With others they are very strict, but for themselves they present many excuses, when it should be the opposite.

Examine yourself with utter precision but try to excuse others. We see the Lord Jesus giving us an example of this when referring to one's sin as "the plank in your eye" and the sin of others as "the speck in your brother's eye" (Matt. 7:3). Thus, you should look at your own mistakes as planks and at others' mistakes as specks. Man's problem in precision is that he divides sin into small and great sins, and then becomes slack with what he calls "small" or "little" sins. What he thinks are small matters are in fact not small at all, for even if they appear small, they will eventually turn into great matters. The spiritual person does not neglect any sin, esteeming it small. To him, all sins are exceedingly sinful and "the wages of sin is death" and separation from God as there is no communion of light with darkness (2 Cor. 6:14). The fault in anything decreases its perfection; any spot on a dress distorts its cleanliness, no matter how small it may be.

A spiritual person is precise in resisting sin, and is cautious not to fall into it. He does not wait for sin to approach him in order to resist. Rather, he avoids it and seals himself so that it cannot enter him. If he is attacked by sin, he is very precise in expelling it. He is meticulous in all his actions, obeying the words of the Apostle, "See then that you walk circumspectly, not as fools but as wise" (Eph. 5:15). Thus, he is strict in every work he does; in the work itself, its means, and results. He is even meticulous in things that, even though are not bad, are not beneficial, like the Apostle says, "All things are lawful for me, but all things are not helpful; all things are lawful for me, but all things do not edify" (1 Cor. 10:23).

The spiritual person is meticulous in all his movements, in his coming and going out, in his voice, and in his walk. In speaking with an elderly person, he is mindful not to raise his voice or interrupt, as the spiritual elder said, "He gently opens and shuts the door." In his speech, he is careful that his jokes do not develop into mockery. He is careful not to develop from telling a story to judging, or move from ordering to controlling, or from leadership to boasting and self-praising.

Thus, a spiritual person is meticulous not to change from objectivity to subjectivity. He accounts for every step that he takes, is not pulled by the common current, and does not move from one place to another without thinking. More importantly, he is meticulous in his relationship with God, keeping His commandments and promises to Him, fulfilling his vows, and giving his tithes and first fruits. He does not negotiate with God nor does he go back on a covenant he took
before Him.

❈ The Devils' Combats ❈

The devil fights precision by calling precision rigidity or inflexibility. By this, he aims to ensure that the spiritual person will not tolerate the term 'rigidity' and will abandon his precision. But what the devil criticizes is pharisaism or literalism, not precision. For flexibility does not mean detachment from values, rather flexibility in carrying out the commandments, not breaking them. So, do not let such words stir you to change your principles.

CHAPTER 14

The Victorious Life

❈ The Importance and Blessing of Victory in the Spiritual Life ❈

A spiritual man is victorious in his spiritual warfare: victorious over the self, the devils, and all materialistic desires. His victories make him worthy of crowns on Judgment Day. That is why some see the Church as divided in two: a church on earth called the Militant Church, and another in heaven called the Victorious Church which, during the period of striving on earth, fought and prevailed.

In the Book of Revelation, the Lord explains to us the blessings received by those who are victorious. In His messages to the seven churches, He repeats the words, "He who overcomes shall be..." or "To him who overcomes I will give...". He says, "To him who overcomes I will give to eat from the tree of life, which is in the midst of the Paradise of God" (2:7). "He who overcomes shall not be hurt by the second death" (2:11). "He who overcomes shall be clothed in white garments, and I will not blot out his name from the Book of Life; but I will confess his name before My Father and before His angels" (3:5). "He who overcomes I will make him a pillar in the temple of My God" (3:12). "To him who overcomes I will grant to sit with Me on My throne, as I also overcame and sat down with My Father on His throne" (3:21).

The Lord prepared all these blessings for those who strive, prevail, and live the life of victory. No one is excluded from this rule, everyone is given the opportunity to strive and prevail in order to be crowned. Hence, we see St. Paul at the time of his departure saying, "I have fought the good fight, I have finished the race, I have kept the faith. Finally there is laid up for me the crown of righteousness, which the Lord, the righteous Judge, will give to me on that Day, and not to me only but also to all who have loved His appearing" (2 Tim. 4:7,8).

This is why God permits spiritual warfare, temptations, and devils. He tests our will to see the extent of our worthiness of His crowns. We see one of the Fathers saying, "No one is crowned except he who prevails. No one prevails except he who fights. No one fights except he who has an enemy." Saint Paul the Apostle also said, "Put on the whole armor of God, that you may be able to stand against the wiles of the devil. For we do not wrestle against flesh and blood, but against principalities, against powers, against the rulers of the darkness of this age, against spiritual hosts of wickedness in the heavenly places" (Eph. 6:11,12).

❈ You are not Alone ❈

God observes our battles and victories, as do all the angels and spirits of the saints. They all witness our struggles and rejoice when we prevail, according to the words of the Holy Bible: "There is joy in the presence of the angels of God over one sinner who repents" (Luke 15:10). God and His angels do not stand quietly while watching our spiritual warfare, rather they provide us with support.

It is true that God permitted the existence of our adversary; yet, He did not give him authority over us. He permitted spiritual warfare but gave us the power to prevail through the Holy Spirit, the work of grace, and the renewal of human nature and its restoration to its former Divine image. God also gave us authority over the devils, for through Him, we are able to trample on every power of the enemy. We mention this blessing every day at the end of the Thanksgiving Prayer, remembering the power which the Lord granted to His pure Apostles as mentioned in the Gospel of Saint Luke, "Behold, I give you authority to trample on serpents and scorpions, and over all the powers of the enemy" (Luke 10:19). The phrase, "all the powers of the enemy," certainly seems comforting when put alongside the words "trample on."

Thus, the devil is not as fearsome as some may think. Even though he may appear as a roaring lion seeking prey to devour, our Lord gave us power over him. Human nature, previously overcome by the devil, regained the spirit of triumph and victory when our Lord defeated the devil after He took flesh and became man.

He granted us to prevail and showed us an image of the conquered devil to teach us not to fear him. He gave our nature the power to cast out demons, our fathers the Apostles saw how the devils were subject to them in the Name of the Lord (Luke 10:17). How beautiful are the Lord's words about the loss of the devil's power, "I saw Satan fall like lightning from heaven" (Luke 10:18). Therefore, do not fear the devils, for they are not more powerful than you, so long as you fight them with the full armor of God (Eph. 6:11). With the power of God working in and through you, the devils will be subject to you and you will overcome them in your warfare. God Who works in you will conquer them, as He said: "In the world you will have tribulation, but be of good cheer, I have overcome the world" (John 16:33). He did not only mean His personal victory over the world, but also His victory through us over the world.

That is why Saint Paul rightly said, "God always leads us in triumph" (2 Cor. 2:14). Yes, He is the ever-victorious Christ who overcame the world, Satan, and death, always leading us in triumph. Moses likewise said, "The Lord will fight for you and you shall hold your peace" (Ex. 14:14). God loves us and He desires that we live a life of victory. He fights for us while we say with the Apostle, "Yet in all these things, we are more than conquerors through Him who loved us" (Rom. 8:37). It is true that the Lion of the tribe of Judah, the Root of David, has prevailed (Rev. 5:5). Similarly, we will also prevail so long as we abide in Him and receive strength from Him. For He did not give us the spirit of failure, but allowed us to joyfully proclaim, "I can do all things through Christ Who strengthens me" (Phil. 4:13).

Our spiritual warfare is not between us and Satan; it is a war waged by Satan against God and His Kingdom. He fights us as part of his war against the Kingdom of God. This is why God does not allow him to prevail over us. It is His war, as David the Prophet said: "The battle is the Lord's" (1 Sam. 17:47). Moses perceived this when he was fighting the Amalekites and said, "The Lord will have war with Amalek" (Ex. 17:16).

❈ Do Not Despair ❈

Satan attempts to instill a spirit of defeat and weakness in your heart to lead you to despair and submit to him! Do not believe him. He may try to convince you that repentance is difficult, and that a life of righteousness is unattainable in an evil world like ours. He may say to you, "It is futile. Your will is weak, and you will surely fall!" To this, you should respond saying, "It is not my will rather God's work for my sake which matters. And even if I fall, I will surely rise." For the Holy Bible tells us, "A righteous man may fall seven times and rise again" (Prov. 24:16). The prophet also says, "Do not rejoice over me, O my enemy; when I fall I will arise" (Micah 7:8)!

Do not let the fall after every climb agitate you. Rather, rejoice that you rose after every fall. Be assured that God grants you the power to rise, no matter how many times you fall. For, when the Bible mentions falling "Seven times," it means a full number of falls. However, a fall is not a defeat; it is a mere stage from which you rise to become victorious at the end. God knows the power of our enemy and the weakness of our nature. So, He has compassion on our warfare, sending us power to support our weakness and helping us to rise. As we pray to Him in the Divine Liturgy according to St. Gregory, saying, "You have turned my punishment into salvation...As a true Father You travailed with me, I who had fallen...You have bound me with all the remedies that lead to life...You showed me the rising up from my fall."

How beautiful are the words of one of the Fathers who said, "A soldier who is wounded by the enemy is rewarded with medals, not just the soldier who overcomes and kills his enemies." So long as the soldier did not flee from the battle, but fought and struggled, he is rewarded, even if the enemy wounded him. This is not defeat; it is striving.

Put before your eyes the words of the Holy Bible that God "desires all men to be saved and to come to the knowledge of the truth" (1 Tim. 2:4). May you be among those men and be assured of God's good will. If God's help delays in reaching you, do not despair. For, God may come in the fourth watch, yet He will surely come. Saint Augustine's repentance came after many years of sin. But he received salvation at the end, even though it seemed that God's help reached him late! In the same way, we speak of Mary of Egypt, Moses the Black, Saul of Tarsus, and Arianus the governor of Ansena.

God went to prepare a place for us, and He will come to take us to Him (John 14:3). Let us, therefore, be hopeful in the life of victory. "You shall not be afraid of the terror by night, nor of the arrow that flies by day, nor of the pestilence that walks in darkness" (Psa. 90:5,6). Sing with David the Prophet, "Though an army should encamp against me, my heart shall not fear" (Psa. 26:3), for "Though I walk through the valley of the shadow of death, I will fear no evil; for You are with me" (Psa. 22:4). Fill your heart with God's strengthening promises and be assured that you will certainly prevail.

❊ Means of Victory ❊

We mentioned that the most important thing is that God fights in you and for you. Therefore, pour yourself out before him so that He may give you strength and victory. Nevertheless, along with the help of God, you must be on guard.

Avoid the causes of sin and flee from them as much you can. The angel said to Lot, "Escape for your life! Do not look behind you nor stay anywhere in the plain" (Gen. 19:17). Saint Paul the

Apostle says to his disciple Timothy, "Flee also youthful lusts" (2 Tim. 2:22). We also saw how Joseph the Righteous escaped for his life so that he might not fall. One of the Fathers said, "He who is near the object of sin fights two wars: one from the outside and another from the inside. But he who is far from it, is tempted only internally." Therefore, determine where your falls come from and abandon their causes, remembering the words of the Holy Bible, "God divided the light from the darkness" (Gen 1:4); "And if your right hand causes you to sin, cut it off and cast it from you" (Matt. 5:30).

Be precise in your life and guard yourself, even from things which seem small. The Holy Bible tells us, "Catch us the foxes, the little foxes that spoil the vine" (Song 2:15). As one of the Fathers said, "Do not converse with someone whom the devil uses to fight you."

To be victorious, fight with all your might and do not surrender in your warfare. Rebuke evil thoughts; do not entertain them nor leave them to grow within you. Resist lusts and bad desires and do not think of putting them into practice, however pressing they may be. Saint Paul the Apostle rebukes the Hebrews saying, "You have not yet resisted to bloodshed, striving against sin" (Heb. 12:4). Your escape from sin, your striving against it, and your precision are proof that you declare that you are cleaving to God and that your will is good. This encourages grace to work in you.

To be victorious, you must strengthen the love of God in your heart by being regular in the means of grace. Most of those who fall are far from the means of grace: prayer, contemplation, reading, fasting, spiritual gatherings, confession, and Holy Communion. Cleave to these means of grace. Always be mindful of God and let the spiritual feelings that keep you away from sin fill your heart.

Let your spiritual principles be sound and let your goal be God and His Kingdom. Know that the more goals you have, the more they will overwhelm your emotions and pull you away from God.

You cannot worship two masters: God and your worldly aims. Always try to give your depths to God alone, and if ever other aims begin to creep into your heart, be alert and reject them.

If you want to be victorious, always guard your heart with humility. Humility makes you seek guidance, depending not on your own understanding. Humility makes you confess your sins and gives you contrition of heart, inviting God to draw near you with His grace and help. Humility makes you pray, asking for God to intervene in your life, instead of depending on your own intelligence and capabilities.

Always feel that you are a beginner. This feeling prompts you to advance and grow. Those whose growth stopped, their fervor ceased, they became lukewarm and weak, and were liable to fall.

CHAPTER 15

Light and Darkness

❈ Separating Light from Darkness ❈

He who begins a spiritual path with God should cut all his ties to sin and its causes. He should avoid all bad companionship, obeying the words of the Holy Bible, "For what fellowship has righteousness with lawlessness? And what communion has light with darkness? And what accord has Christ with Belial? Or what part has a believer with an unbeliever" (2 Cor. 6:14,15).

A spiritual person must separate himself from all things sinful or tempting, as he cannot possess both love for God and the world. This point is clear since the beginning of creation, the Divine Inspiration says, "Then God said: 'Let there be light and there was light. And God saw the light, that it was good; and God divided the light from the darkness" (Gen. 1:3,4). This image remained an established principle by which God dealt with His children for many generations.

Let us consider the spreading of evil throughout the world before the Flood. The Ark separated Noah and his children from all the wrong companionship of the evil world. It was a symbol of this "separation of light and darkness" principle, saving Noah and his family from
the wrath of God and the perdition that descended on the world.

The same happened with our father Abraham. At the beginning of his calling, God said to him: "Get out of your country, from your kindred and from your father's house, to a land that I will show you" (Gen. 12:1). Thus, Abraham was separated from the paganism that existed at his time, becoming estranged in a holy land where he could worship God and live in righteousness. When Abraham walked against this spiritual rule, he suffered. When he went to the land of Gerar, he faced a severe temptation from Abimelech from which God intervened to save him (Gen. 20). Similarly, when he went to Egypt during the famine, God miraculously saved him from an ordeal with Pharaoh (Gen. 12:14-20). In these two events, Abraham learned a lesson.

In a more dangerous way, the same befell Lot in the land of Sodom. His living in an evil environment caused him spiritual trouble. The Apostle Peter said about him, "for that righteous man dwelling among them, tormented his righteous soul from day to day by seeing and hearing their lawless deeds" (2 Peter 2:8). He was eventually taken captive and the country was burnt by the wrath of God. He was saved by a Divine miracle through the intercession of our father Abraham who was far away from the fellowship of evil and evildoers.

❦ A Divine and Ecclesial Commandment ❦

God laid down the spiritual laws necessary to separate His people from sinful companionship, among which was the forbiddance of intermarriage with foreign women. Solomon the Wise deviated from the path of God when he fell into this sin. Foreign women drew his heart towards worshipping other gods to the extent that he erected high places "for all his foreign wives, who burned incense and sacrificed to their gods" (1 Kings 11:1-8). Solomon turned many times to correct this error, as mentioned in the Book of Proverbs (2: 16, 7:5, 5:20, 6:24, 22:14).

Saint Paul the Apostle laid for us an important spiritual principle when he said, "Do not be deceived; Evil company corrupts good habits" (1 Cor. 15:33), "not to keep company with sexually immoral people"
(1 Cor. 5:9), and "put away from yourselves that wicked person" (1 Cor. 5:13). He explicitly said, "not to keep company with anyone named a brother, who is a fornicator, or covetous, or an idolater,

or a reviler, or a drunkard, or an extortioner - not even to eat with such a person" (1 Cor. 5:11). The same advice is given in the first Psalm, "Blessed is the man who walks not in the counsel of the ungodly, nor stands in the path of sinners, nor sits in the seat of the scornful" (Psa. 1:1).

Man is influenced by the environment that surrounds him. Thus, it is better to flee from all sinful surroundings. For this reason, the Church, during Her early generations, would excommunicate sinners from the communion of the believers, utterly forbidding their presence inside the Church. She imposed very strict ecclesiastical canons during the early centuries such that church attendance was exclusively for holy people. Attending the Liturgy of the Catechumens was permitted to new believers, not sinners. After attending the readings of the epistles, the Acts of the Apostles, the Synaxarion, the Gospel, and the sermon, these catechumens had to leave the Church.

This excommunication was not exclusive to those who sinned through behavior, but also those who deviated from the faith and dogma. Regarding this, Saint John the Beloved said, "If anyone comes to you and does not bring this doctrine, do not receive him into your house nor greet him; for he who greets him shares in his evil deeds" (2 John 1:10,11). This was done to prevent the schismatics and heretics from spreading their beliefs among the congregation of believers and influencing them. Saint John's advice may also be useful nowadays to face those who spread skepticism in religion such as atheists, Jehovah's Witnesses, or whoever spreads ideas contrary to the faith that was once delivered to the saints (Jude 3).

The most famous example of excommunication during the Apostolic Era was that of Ananias and Sapphira. Saint Peter did not accept the couple's lying to the Holy Spirit of God (Acts 5:1-11). Another important example was the punishment given by Saint Paul the Apostle to the sinner of Corinth (1 Cor. 5:1-5). However, the oldest example of excommunication was the expulsion of Adam and Eve from Paradise, separating them from the Tree of

Life. While sin is a separation from God, His Kingdom, and His angels and saints, the life of righteousness is a separation from sin and the fellowship of sinners.

In Baptism, a spiritual person begins his separation from sin by renouncing Satan together with his evil deeds, unclean spirits, authority, and the rest of his hypocrisies. He is separated from his old man, which dies in baptism; then a new man is born according to the Image of God. He is separated from all sins committed before baptism, living a new, pure life, abiding in God and fulfilling the words of the Holy Bible, "God divided the light from the darkness."

❈ A More Serious Separation in Eternity ❈

Just as there is a separation here on earth between light and darkness, there will also be a more profound separation in the age to come. This is made clear in the story of the rich man and Lazarus, when our father Abraham said to the rich man, "And besides all this, between us and you there is a great gulf fixed, so that those who want to pass from here to you cannot, nor can those from there pass to us" (Luke 16:26).

On the fearful Day of Judgment, there will be a separation between those on the right and those on the left. God will separate the sheep from the goat, the wheat from the tares, and the righteous from the wicked. They will no longer live together as was the case on earth. The righteous will enjoy the eternal bliss and dwell in the land of the living, while the wicked will be thrown to the outer darkness, into the fire prepared for Satan and his evil spirits.

Here, on earth, any sinner can meet a saint, shake his hands, sit and talk with him, and ask for his prayers. But, in eternity, sinners will not be able to meet the saints. The rich man will not be able to sit with Lazarus; rather he will either watch him from afar or not at all. The sinners' deprivation of the communion of the angels and saints will be part of their eternal suffering. It is the separation between light and darkness intended by God since the moment of Creation.

Therefore, if you love someone and care about their eternal life, there is one piece of advice for you: Both of you should live a life acceptable to God so that you can be together in eternity. But if you walk different paths regarding righteousness and holiness, you will never meet in eternity. Living a sinful life on earth, you will be consumed by affliction in eternity and will be prevented from enjoying each other's company. Care for your eternal life and love for God and do not forfeit your soul, even if you cannot meet your loved ones in eternity.

❀ How to Separate from Darkness? ❀

If you cannot separate yourself from sinners, at least separate yourself from their ways. If you have to live in an unspiritual environment and you cannot physically separate yourself from sinners, then separate yourself in heart and in mind. For most of the world is not spiritual and you cannot leave the world as our teacher Saint Paul said. Therefore, separate your heart from every evil lust, your mind from every sinful thought, and your senses (as best you can) from seeing and listening to what offends you spiritually.

Remember the words of Saint Paul the Apostle, "and those who use this world as not misusing it" (1 Cor. 7:31). Listen to his saying, "And do not be conformed to this world" (Rom.12:2), that is, do not change and become in its image and likeness. Become distinguished by your spiritual ways, as Saint John the Beloved said, "Whoever has been born of God does not sin, for His seed remains in him; and he cannot sin, because he has been born of God. In this way the children of God and the children of the devil are manifest" (1 John 3:9,10).

The children of God have transcended the world and its lusts, concentrating all their love on God alone. They reject the stance which Elijah criticized when he said: "How long will you falter between two opinions? If the Lord is God, follow Him; but if Baal then follow him" (1 Kings 18:21). A true believer does not try to combine both God and the world, giving one hour to prayer and another to worldly pleasures, without being steadfast in either condition.

The Holy Bible says, "You shall love the Lord your God with all your heart, with all your soul, and with all your might" (Deut. 6:5). The term, "with all," means that there is no other love beside God competing with Him, and that there is no darkness sharing His marvelous light within you. Your separation from darkness does not only involve the passive side but also the positive side, according to the words of the Apostle, "And have no fellowship with the unfruitful works of darkness, but rather expose them" (Eph. 5:11).

Exposing darkness refers to your rejection of darkness inside you or anybody else, showing your care for God's kingdom and its spread. Exposing darkness signifies the strength of the heart, for it does not grow weak before the prince of darkness (Luke 22:53). It is a heart that confronts and resists darkness in the same manner as Elijah who stood against King Ahab and the prophets of Baal (1 King 18), and as John the Baptist who stood against Herod and Herodias (Matt. 14:3,4).

You are light and sin is darkness; but light is capable of extinguishing all darkness. You are light because the Lord Jesus Christ said to us, "You are the light of the world" (Matt. 5:14), and said afterwards, "Let your light so shine before men, that they may see your good works and glorify your Father in heaven" (Matt. 5:16). When your light shines, darkness disperses, it will not overshadow your light, rather your light will expel it.

Do you have this high spiritual presence which disperses darkness from around you? Does your mere presence make people around you unable to utter idle or unsuitable words, or unable to behave in an inappropriate manner? Does your presence make them feel that you bring the presence of God to them? Then, they will say to you, "We knew God the day we knew you." Do you merely separate yourself from darkness or do you also overcome it? Are you a lamp that is placed on a lampstand, giving light to all who are in the house, such that there is no darkness (Matt. 5:15)? Are you a candle that is lit, casting out the darkness?

Your light can be your teaching; that is good. But what is better is for your life to be a light that illuminates the way for others. However, you can never be light unless you love light, and you can never disperse darkness unless you despise it from the depths of your heart. Therefore, examine your heart thoroughly and disperse from it all darkness. If the love of God enters your heart, the love of the world and sin will be expelled from it.

You must be certain that sin is darkness. You cannot commit sin except in darkness, in secret, without being noticed by people. And if anyone exposes you, you try to cover it up with excuses, justifications, lies, or by accusing others so that it remains in darkness and no one sees it except you.

So long as God is light, then sin, which is darkness, separates you from life with God. As the Apostle said, "What communion has light with darkness?" (2 Cor. 6:14). If the righteous will rise on the last Day with a spiritual, illumined body and will shine as snow, and all those who turn many to righteousness will shine like the stars forever and ever (Dan. 12:3), what shall we say about those who lived in darkness? They will be cast into outer darkness, for how will they have an illumined spirit?

In this manner, God has separated light from darkness in eternity as well. This is not merely in terms of place —for the righteous will live in the city of light that has no need of the sun or moon because the glory of God illumines it (Rev. 21:23), but also in terms of the nature of spirits. The spirits of the righteous will be illumined and those of the sinners will be dark. It is impossible for the spirits of the sinners to be illumined because they have separated themselves from God who is the True Light. Thus, they will live in the outer darkness where there is no communion between light and darkness.

CHAPTER 16

The Life of Submission

To live a life of submission is to place your life in the hands of God and forget it there, having full trust that He will manage it well according to His blessed will. This requires trust in God and faith in His love, wisdom, and care. Unfortunately, however, most people trust in their self, intelligence, ideas, and human plans more than they trust in God. They thus manage their affairs on their own, without thinking of turning to God or depending on him as the life of submission requires.

What causes a person much toil and exhaustion is for him to turn away from God and depend on himself. For then, he is led by the self, its desires, lusts, and thoughts or is even led by other people. His dependence on God is only partial and within certain limits, it is a dependence that lacks depth, is untrusting, hesitant, and leads to doubt, fear, or lack of assurance. This reminds me of Saint Peter when he walked with Christ on the water but became afraid and began to drown. He deserved the rebuke of the Lord when He said, "O you of little faith, why did you doubt?" (Matt. 14:31).

We see the opposite example in the Israelites who walked in the midst of the Red Sea while the waters surrounded them on both sides. They certainly had their life submitted to God with full trust in Him. Some contemplate and say that the most submissive in this incident was he who first placed his foot in the water after Moses had struck it, trusting that it would certainly part. Similarly when they walked under the pillar of clouds, not knowing where they were going, but trusting that the Lord would lead them. Like them also, was our father Noah when he entered the ark with the beasts. He left the sailing of the boat to the Lord, trusting that He would carry him out of it onto dry land after the flood.

Our father Adam did not live a life of submission. Instead, he followed his own desires, those of his wife and the serpent, abandoning God and His commandment. He allowed the desire for knowledge to lead him astray; and it led him to ignorance and death! Jonah the prophet did not live the life of submission either. He fled from God and was angered by His divine will unto death (Jonah 4). Even King Saul, his perdition was because he turned away from God and followed his own thoughts and impulses, sometimes even turning to soothsayers.

A life of submission, as we have said, is the submission of your life to God and to His work in you. It is submitting to the work of grace, the work of the Holy Spirit, and the good will of God. It resembles the relationship between the sheep and their shepherd. When he leads, they follow, fully trusting in his leadership and having no other thoughts or opinion. It is absolute obedience that is based on absolute trust.

❈ Characteristics ❈

A life of submission, then, is tied to obedience. We mean true obedience, without grumbling, complaining, or having two wills. You obey God with a joyful heart, having no will apart from His, saying, "I have no other thought, opinion, or desire, but to follow You." The reason for any fall is this dualism of wills between your own and that of God.

The Lord guided us to the life of submission when He taught us to say, in the Lord's prayer, "Your will be done." May our will be His will and His will become ours. Let us not allow our will to be different from His. A person who possesses this unity of will cannot sin, for he is in communion with the Holy Spirit and cannot resist or oppose the Divine will. This is one of the fruits of the life of submission.

Consequently, stubbornness can be a form of sin, as it contradicts a life of submission. The one who lives a life of submission "does not sin; but he who has been born of God keeps himself, and the wicked one does not touch him" (1 John 5:18). In this manner, "the children of God are manifest" (1 John 3:10). The one who lives the life of submission submits everything to God—his heart, thoughts, and senses—and does not try to intervene in God's work within him. He submits his desires, emotions, and reactions to Him. This is the true submission of which St. Paul spoke of saying, "It is no longer I who live, but Christ who lives in me" (Gal. 2:20). It is crucifying one's self such that it no longer resists God's will.

The one who lives a life of submission asks the Lord in every situation, "Lord, what do You want me to do?" (Acts 9:6). "I cannot choose for myself, so I always ask for what You choose for me. If I choose for myself, I may err. I do not believe in my own wisdom, but You know what is good for me." Such a person follows the words of the Scriptures, "lean not on your own understanding" (Prov. 3:5) because "There is a way that seems right to a man, but its end is the way of death" (Prov. 14:12, 16:25). He says to God: "For this reason, I leave this matter to Your divine providence and submit it to You. For You, my Lord, see what I do not see and know what I do not know. You know what is good for me and will lead me to green pastures and the springs of living water."

Therefore, a life of submission must be built upon the humility and simplicity of the heart. It relies on self-denial; for anyone who depends on himself, his capabilities, or knowledge will struggle to submit to God. Those who analyze the will of God and His work in their lives, using it as a source of arguing and debating, will not be able to attain the life of submission. These are called the "intellectual ones."

Abraham, the father of the patriarchs, lived a life of submission as he left his family and was willing to offer his son as a burnt offering to the Lord. He left his family and homeland, not knowing where he was going. He submitted his life to the Lord to lead him wherever He wishes. In like manner, he took his only son to offer him as a burnt sacrifice, submitting to the power of God which is able to raise the dead (Heb. 11).

The one who lives a life of submission submits the aim, means, and result to God. He lets God choose for him the path and the way, accepting anything that comes from Him. And so, he lives in a state of constant joy and satisfaction. For sorrow comes when a person sets a goal for himself and does not achieve it. But the one who lives a life of submission does not place desires before him, instead, he leaves the Lord to guide his path. As Jeremiah the prophet said, "O Lord, I know the way of man is not in himself; It is not in man who walks to direct his own steps" (Jer. 10:23). The one who submits his ways to the Lord never worries because he trusts that God will prosper his ways. The one who leads himself, however, worries.

St. Paul the Apostle submitted his life to the Lord, hence we see him singing and praising while he was in prison (Acts 16). Nothing bothered or worried him. He even wrote some of his epistles during that period. Likewise, St. Peter the apostle slept comfortably in prison while death awaited him the next day (Acts 12). The life of submission led him to reassurance, even in the most difficult of times.

This reminds me of the sick patient who calmly and trustingly lays down, submitting his body to the surgeon's scalpel. "For He bruises, but He binds up." In his sleep and submission, he does not try to move, nor does he ask the surgeon what he is doing. It is enough for him that he is in the hands of a trusted person that desires what is good for him, trusting those hands are sufficient.

This applies to all those who followed God in submission. They neither asked nor argued, much like what happened in the calling of our fathers the apostles. Matthew, when he was in the collection office and received the call, left everything and did not ask "Where to?" Peter and Andrew, John, and his brother James all left their nets and fishing, following Christ without knowing where they were headed; they did not ask. This is the life of submission.

God chose those who lived a life of submission knowing that they had simple and ready hearts that trust and do not try to search out things in a stubbornness often labeled as knowledge or wisdom. For this reason, the Lord Jesus Christ said, "I thank You, Father, Lord of heaven and earth, that You have hidden these things from the wise and prudent and revealed them to babes" (Luke 10:21), meaning those who are simple. It is as if the believer says to the Lord in all his problems: "I present them to You, Lord. I have fasted and prayed. I submit everything to You, trusting that You will act. How or when I do not know, but what I know for sure is that You will do what is good. I will see Your work, whether now or after some time. I will look upon this matter with hope, faith, love, and trust, remembering the many experiences I have had under Your care."

Thus, a person who lives a life of submission is not anxious about time. He knows God will act in the fitting time. For God's supposed delay is only a matter of the way man thinks about time. In the life of submission, leave time to God, for He knows best what the right time is. Trust in His work, no matter how much the devil plagues you with despair or tells you, "There's no use." If you have submitted everything into the hands of God, then you have submitted it into the hands of the Almighty, the lover of mankind, maker of all things, the fullness of wisdom and knowledge, and the one who has engraved you on the palm of His hand.

Truly, these characteristics of God are beautiful, urging a person even more to a life of submission and reassurance. For regardless of any obstacles a person may be facing, he can trust in God and His promises. God is constantly working, even though it may seem at times that everything has stopped. In the life of submission, do not depend on your feelings or personal intuitions. If you ask something of the Lord, believe that He is working even before you asked Him.

The apostles lived the life of submission in their preaching and service. They went to countries they had never been to before and did not speak their languages. Those countries did not have churches, believers, or any other resources, but living the life of submission, they trusted that God will manage the affairs of the service and prosper it. They did not even ask, "How?"

Our fathers, the anchorites and spirit-borne, lived a life of submission. They lived without any human help, wandering in the deserts and barren lands. Many of them lived tens of years without seeing a human face. Yet, they were happy with their lives having submitted them to the Lord. Many generations witnessed how the Lord took care of such people both physically and spiritually in this life of submission they experienced.

The one who lives the life of submission is not overwhelmed and does not worry. He has cast all his cares on the Lord from the moment that he submitted his life to Him, knowing that the One Who cares for all, cares for him also. Why are you so filled with cares if your Heavenly Father knows all your needs and shepherds you so that you need nothing? "Do not worry about tomorrow, for tomorrow will worry about its own things" (Matt. 6:34). The God of tomorrow will take care of everything just as He did all the days prior.

It is beautiful how we hear in the story of John the Baptist that an angel took him to the wilderness in his childhood in order to save him. Or Phillip who baptized the Ethiopian Eunuch and the Spirit of the Lord caught him away and he was found at Azotus (Acts 8). There is also the story of St. Macarius the Great who grew weary on his journey in the wilderness and said, "Lord, You know that I do not possess any more strength." At once, he found himself in Shiheet.

The Spirit of God who guided the fathers beforetime is also able to lead you if you submit your life to Him. Those fathers entered the life of submission, experienced the Lord, and tasted Him. As a result, their faith was strengthened, and they were able to delve deeper into the life of submission. Every day, they underwent new trials; and with every trial, they grew stronger in submission. Thus, the more they submitted, the more they experienced. Grace led them to grace.

By submission, you will live in peace. For with many cares, comes much worry. How long will you continue to carry heavy burdens that bend your back? Cast it on
God. Is He not the One Who said, "Come to Me, all you who labor and are heavy laden, and I will give you rest" (Matt. 11:28). Is it too much for God—Who carried all the burdens of the world from Adam until now and until the end of the ages—to carry your burden?

A person can stay in Church, trying to resolve his worries and anxieties rather than leave it all to God. He carries the burdens of God, if this expression can be accurate! Why, my son, do you exhaust yourself? Why do you weary yourself with talking so much about all that worries you? Submit all your matters to the Lord, Who carries you and the Church, without worrying.

It is good to experience the Lord that you may speak about Him to your children, descendants, and disciples. You will not merely speak about the God of the Scriptures and holy books, but about the God of your life, the One you experienced and tasted, the God of every day and every moment. You will talk about God who never neglects His children. The One about Whom David the prophet said, "Even if my father and mother forsake me, the Lord will hold me close" (Psa. 26:10).

Poor are those who have not tasted the Lord. How can you taste Him? By experience. How do you experience Him? By entering into the life of submission. Submit your life to Him in the same manner that a child gives his hand to his father, to lead him through a crowd in a busy city. Or like a child that rests his head on his mother's shoulder and feels the fullness of security, rest, and peace.

Let us go back, then, to the life of spiritual childhood, in its simplicity, trust, submission, and peace, for "Unless you are converted and become as little children, you will by no means enter the kingdom of heaven" (Matt. 18:3). Children live a life of submission, trusting their parents and teachers more than themselves.

In the life of submission, do not argue or complain, but trust that God carries it all. Try the life of submission and all that it entails in terms of joy, reassurance, and peace. Attain for yourself spiritual experience by submitting your life to the Lord. One of the saints once meditated on the saying "We have left all and followed You" and said, "Our leaving all things and following Him is leaving behind our identities and wills." Pray and say, "Lord, I have stayed up all night and caught nothing. But, in the life of submission, and in Your Name, I will cast the nets." So trust that they will be filled with fish; for God Who created the sea will fill them.

CHAPTER 17

The Life of Thanksgiving

Imagine we are at the start of a new year. What do you see us asking God for? People have grown accustomed to asking for what they desire. There is nothing wrong with that, but what is wrong is that there are very few people who thank God for His gracious gifts during the previous year. Or, if they do thank Him, it is very little in comparison to their requests.

One of the spiritual fathers once said, "There is no talent without increase, except the one without thanksgiving." For this reason, I would like to speak in this section about thanksgiving, that it may be a significant component of our prayers on New Year's Eve. It is a shame that we make new requests every year, without giving thanks for what we have received.

❧ Things to be Thankful For ❧

Be thankful for God's goodness to you, your relatives, your loved ones, the church, and the community that you live in. You will undoubtedly find many positive things that are deserving of gratitude. At least, sit with yourself and try to remember all that the Lord has done for you and your loved ones. Do this not only for this past year, but also for all the previous years, even for your entire life.

Thank God that He does not treat you based on the way that you treat Him, that He does not punish you for the multitude of sins that you see in yourself. Rather, He has covered you, helped you, opened His House for you, and granted you His Mysteries. Do not think that your thanksgiving to God is limited for the miracles He has performed but include even the finest details of your life and be thankful for them.

❈ Church Teaching ❈

The Church teaches us to give thanks for many things, some of which we would not think we should be thankful for, but the Book of Hours reminds us to. In the prayer of the Eleventh Hour, we pray saying, "We thank You, our compassionate King, for You have granted us to pass this day in peace and brought us to the evening thankfully, and made us worthy to behold daylight until evening." And in the prayer of the First Hour, we say, "We thank You, O King of ages, for You have let us pass through the night in peace and brought us to the daybreak." What is this wondrous sensitivity and thanksgiving? We thank God for every minute that we live, considering it a gift from God that we have been granted in order to do good.

Our standing for prayer is something that we should thank God for because He has granted us the opportunity to speak with Him. He bestowed upon us the grace to be freed from all the cares of this world and stand before Him, especially in holy times. This is why the Church teaches us to say, "in this holy hour in which You abundantly poured the grace of Your Holy Spirit...". The phrase "raised us up" means that we feel that grace is what has moved us to pray and helped us to do so, it was not the result of our own will, which if we left to its own devices, we most likely would not have prayed.

The Church teaches us to begin our prayers with thanksgiving. This is not only in the prayers of the Agpeya, but also at the beginning of the Divine Liturgy and every other mystery. Even when we pray over those who have reposed, we start with the Thanksgiving Prayer.

We say in the Thanksgiving Prayer, "We thank You for every condition, concerning every condition, and in every condition." It is a prayer of the life of submission, where we prove our trust that "all things work together for good to those who love God" (Rom. 8:28). Perhaps this phrase is taken from the verse in the Bible that says, "giving thanks always for all things" (Eph. 5:20). It is a lesson for those who love complaining, are continually discontent, or are worried with many things. In a life of faith, we are thankful for everything, saying, "We will give thanks no matter what happens to us. All is for good."

❖ Thanking God for Blessings and Tribulations ❖

Most people give thanks for blessings but very few give thanks in times of tribulation. He who loves God thanks Him during tribulations. He cannot complain about what God has permitted, but trusts in His care, help, and goodness, believing that his trial will end in what is good for him.

What is higher than giving thanks during a time of tribulation is giving thanks for the tribulation itself. Giving thanks in trials is connected to the virtue of endurance or submission, recognizing the tribulation, but being thankful for it, nonetheless. For if God allowed it, why do we not allow it for ourselves? To give thanks for tribulations, however, is to love tribulations. Similar to the disciples who were imprisoned and beaten, but they "rejoiced that they were counted worthy to suffer shame for His name" (Acts 5:41). Another example is the saying of St. James the apostle, "My brethren, count it all joy when you fall into various trials" (James 1:2). Naturally, a person who thanks God for hardship will be thankful for graces and blessings as well.

Let us ask ourselves then: do we thank God for all His gifts or are there hidden gifts for which we do not thank God, gifts that we forget and do not remember? You might thank God for delivering you from a certain trial, but how about the other trials that would have befallen you if it was not for God's prevention. Perhaps there was a sin meant to attack you, but God prevented this temptation from you. Maybe the devil intended to weaken your faith, but the Lord rebuked him, and he could not approach you. Meanwhile, you are unaware and do not give thanks.

The Lord who commanded us to do good in secret also does good for us in secret. The good that He openly does for us allows us to experience His love. We love because He first loved us. Thus, no matter how much we may thank God, we will never be able to give Him His due. It is enough that He made our bodies as temples and permitted His Holy Spirit to dwell and work in us (1 Cor. 3:16; 6:19). It is enough that He allowed Himself to be our Father and that we be His children. St. John says about this, "Behold what manner of love the Father has bestowed on us, that we should be called children of God!" (1 John 3:1). Therefore, let us be thankful for everything: both spiritual and material gifts, the seen and unseen.

Most importantly, we should be thankful for trials, for they are also gifts. Let us pray within ourselves, saying: "I thank You, Lord, from the depths of my heart for this illness because it has drawn me closer to You. It allowed me to return to prayer, to examine myself, and to blame it for its sins. I am thankful for this illness because of all the love that You have surrounded me with at this time. Because it has granted me time to retreat and be alone with You, because it gave me the blessing of pain, and revealed to me how I failed to visit the sick. It has also prepared me for eternity. Truly, how numerous are the blessings of this illness! How fitting it is to be thankful for it."

❖ Obstacles to Thanksgiving ❖

† *Pessimism.* Sometimes we do not give thanks because we do not focus on the positive aspects of our lives, but only on the hardships. This can lead to sorrow, worry, complaining, and pessimism, all of which leave no room for thanksgiving. I would like you to start a new year with joy. Remember all the joyful things about the past year and give thanks for them.

† *Misattribution.* Sometimes we do not give thanks because we ascribe the joyful things in our life to something other than God. If we pass our exams, we ascribe it to our own intelligence, the diligence of our teachers, or the simplicity

of the exam. However, God's help is hidden in all this. In like manner, if we are healed, we give credit to the doctors. If we are promoted in our job, we ascribe it to our own skills and merits. If we are saved from an accident, we give credit to the skill of the driver. We hide God from the reasons for our joy, and do not give thanks for anything.

✝ *Taking Things for Granted*. Sometimes we do not give thanks for something unless we lose it. We do not feel that blessed until that blessing is taken away from us. We do not thank God for the presence of our parents or feel how blessed we are with them until one of them reposes. We are not thankful for our health or know its value until we fall ill. We do not realize the blessing of there being light in a room unless there is a power outage.

✝ *Belittling*. Sometimes we do not give thanks because we feel that it is too small or insignificant of a matter to give thanks for. Here, we mention one of the sayings of the spiritual fathers, "He is a liar who claims that he gives thanks for much, when he does not give thanks for the little." Perhaps, we view it as something natural or ordinary and therefore do not feel the need to be thankful for it. Why do we not give thanks for the beautiful, natural things? Why do we not thank God for the beauty of nature? Why do we not thank Him for good weather? Are we waiting for it to turn bad and then feel like we lost something?

✝ *Preoccupation, Impure Hearts*. We often rejoice over gifts but become satisfied with this joy and do not give thanks. We are happy about the good things that we have without giving thanks for them. It is like a student who is happy about his success, a young woman about her engagement, an employee with his promotion, but without any of them giving thanks to God. God is not in need of our thanksgiving, rather we are the ones who need it. Why? By giving thanks, we remember God's goodness and love for us. By doing so, we abide more in Him and grow in our love for Him, both which are spiritually beneficial for us. This gratitude or thanksgiving also points to the purity of our hearts. The one who lacks gratitude is unaware of his blessings and does not appreciate the one who blessed him.

† *Habit.* Sometimes we do not give thanks because we are not accustomed to doing so. Concerning gifts, we forget the giver and do not give thanks to Him. If we do not thank other people for their services to us, then naturally, we will not thank God. As the Apostle said, "he who does not love his brother whom he has seen, how can he love God whom he has not seen" (1 John 4:20). The same thing can be said about thanksgiving. Therefore, accustom yourself to always give thanks for everything, even if it seems like a small or insignificant matter. Say within yourself, "I thank You, Lord, that You have sent this person to help me and granted him the strength to serve me." This way, you thank both God and people simultaneously. You thank your human brother for his visible act towards you and God for preparing this service for you in an invisible manner. Training ourselves in thanksgiving will ingrain in our minds valuable ideas. The first of which is that everything good is a gift from God: life, health, work, jobs, money, everything. Since it is a gift, we must thank the giver for it.

† *Selfishness.* Sometimes, we do not give thanks because of our own selfishness. We only think of ourselves. If we are granted something, we are satisfied, but do not consider the hand that gave it to us. It is like a hungry person before whom food is placed, he eats it without thinking who gave it to him or thinking about thanking him. Likewise, we tend to only take and not give thanks. If God opens for a person a door for a job or some other source of income, he becomes preoccupied with it, with succeeding and maintaining it, neglecting to thank God for granting him

this gift.

- † *Arrogance and Pride.* We do not thank about things that we claim are personal or natural circumstances. In this case, we are confusing gifts for the self. You think well, but you do not give thanks for the gift of thought which God granted you. You do not give thanks for intelligence and understanding. You do not say with the psalmist, "I will bless the Lord who has given me counsel" (Psa. 15:7). Do not think that intelligence is something of yourself, it is a gift of God and is worthy of thanksgiving. In like manner is any other gift, be it poetry, music, beauty, strength, or your spiritual life.

- † *Ignorance.* Sometimes we do not give thanks because we do not understand the wisdom of God. There are many things that we go through, but do not give thanks for. Instead, we get upset and complain about them. This is because we do not understand God's wisdom in their occurrence, if we did, we would give thanks to God for them. Thus, it is our own fault. We have eyes, but do not see the good in what we go through. Joseph the Righteous, when he was sold and later thrown into prison, did not understand God's wisdom. He did not see it at the time, but later realized that it was for his good.

- † *Discontent, Dissatisfaction.* Sometimes we do not give thanks for what is good because of comparison. We do not give thanks for what God has given us because we see that others have what is more or better than us, or that someone has undeservedly received the same as us. An example of this is an employee in a company who receives a salary higher than what he had initially expected, one that is double or triple that of his coworkers. However, this employee is not thankful because he only looks at the people in the company who earn more than him. Thus, he does not thank God. If you must compare, compare yourself to he who is lesser than you and thank God for his blessings.

Do not compare yourself to someone who is higher than you so you do not complain. Do not be like a millionaire who does not thank God because there are billionaires in the world, and instead feels that what he has is very little, insignificant, and is not at all worthy of thanksgiving.

✝ *Ambition.* There are those who are not thankful because of ambition. They constantly seek to be in a higher status, desiring more than what they possess. So long as they are directed by these ambitions, everything they have will feel so small in their eyes and they will not give thanks for it. Ambition in a moderate matter, and not that of worldly lusts and desires, is not a sin, but ambition should not prevent thanksgiving. Thank God for what you have and you will be given more. Ambition should not lead you to belittle what God has granted you. If you aspire to be a university professor, this does not mean that you should not thank God for placing you in an educational institution and helping you reach the position of associate professor. There are many who fall prey to sinful ambitions, forget God, and live in sorrow and complaining. Spiritual ambition, however, does not fall victim, so long as one lives a life of humility, thanking God, and seeking to be filled with His love.

✝ *Sin and Selfishness.* Some do not give thanks as a result of having a nature of complaining, greed, or love of the world. Such people live in sin, they do not abide in God nor profess His goodness to them. All they care about are the pleasures of the world. As the Scriptures say, "All the rivers run into the sea, yet the sea is not full" (Ecc. 1:7). Be happy with what you have and thank God for it. Do not seek to fill not only your hands, but also your pockets and safes. For greed prevents thanksgiving, and if a person is not accustomed to contentment, it will be difficult for him to live a life of thanksgiving.

✝ *A Weak Spiritual Life.* Sometimes the lack of thanksgiving results from a weak spiritual life overall. A person may not thank God because he does not have a relationship with God at all. He does not pray the thanksgiving prayer, read the Bible, attend spiritual meetings, or have any relation with God. Such people need to enter a life with God. Then, they will be thankful for knowing Him and for all His gifts.

❈ Virtues Related to Thanksgiving ❈

Virtues are interconnected and related to one another in the same manner that sins are.

✝ Thanksgiving is connected to contentment; those who live a life of contentment always give thanks.

✝ Thanksgiving is related to humility; the humble person feels that he does not deserve anything and is thankful for everything no matter how small.

✝ Thanksgiving is related to faith; by faith, a person trusts that God protects, helps, loves, and makes everything good for him.

✝ Thanksgiving is tied to joy and peace, for they both produce it. The more a person's heart is filled with gratitude, the more peaceful and joyful he becomes. Likewise, if he has joy and peace in his heart, he will be thankful. Through gratitude, a person is saved from many illnesses and problems related to complaining and lack of thankfulness.

So, let us start this year with thanksgiving and may it be a happy year for us, our church, and our country.

CHAPTER 18

The Narrow Path

One of the characteristics of the spiritual life is that it is entered by the narrow path. This is the teaching of the Lord Himself, "Enter by the narrow gate…Because narrow is the gate and difficult is the way which leads to life, and there are few who find it" (Matt. 7:13,14). Therefore, one must toil for the sake of the Lord, sacrifice, endure, and not look for rest, following the example of the poor man Lazarus and not his rich contemporary.

The tribulations that you endure are signs of your genuine love for God and your readiness to sacrifice everything for Him. Your entire life on earth is a test for you. Do you prioritize your eternal life, spirituality, and relationship with God above all else? Are you willing to pay the price? Therefore, trials are a test of how much you cling to God.

Trials and tribulations appear as necessary tests and fundamental signs in one's spiritual path. For what makes you worthy of heaven or of a crown if you have lived a luxurious life of comfort on earth? Do you think you can have both a life of comfort on earth and the same in heaven? Does this not contradict the saying of our father Abraham, "in your lifetime you received your good things" (Luke 16:25).

Therefore, if you find yourself walking in the path of God with ease and constant rest, without tribulations or weariness, ask yourself, "Have I strayed from the path?" It must be so for the path is not easy and without toil. Is there not a devil that wars against us? Are there not obstacles that come from the world and the body? Is there not opposition from the enemies of good? Without a doubt, if the devil is not pleased with your actions, he would not leave you at rest at all! Then, why is he leaving you alone?

It is something to consider. Which of the saints lived their life in complete comfort without toil? None of them. All the saints entered by the narrow gate for the sake of their love for God saying, "For to you it has been granted on behalf of Christ, not only to believe in Him, but also to suffer for His sake" (Phil. 1:29). Therefore, these tribulations and pains whisper into your ear, "Be assured. You are on the right path." In this manner, you should rejoice and be reassured in your trials that you are walking in the way of the Lord.

❖ What are these Tribulations? ❖

First is the opposition of the body to the desires of the spirit, "For the flesh lusts against the Spirit, and the Spirit against the flesh" (Gal. 5:17). A spiritual person should thus enter into a struggle with his body, as St. Paul says, "I discipline my body and bring it into subjection" (1 Cor. 9:27). This period of discipline may be brief for some people and longer for others depending on how strong the opposition is.

May we remember that our first fathers, Adam and Eve, did not enter through the narrow gate when they ate from the tree. Esau, Jacob's brother, did not enter through the narrow gate either when he sold his birthright (Gen. 25:33). In like manner, the children of Israel refused to enter through the narrow gate when they complained about the heavenly food and desired to eat meat (Num. 11:4). The opposite of these examples is Daniel who decided to not be defiled by the king's delicacies and preferred that he and the three holy youth eat vegetables (Dan. 1:8,12).

This is why spiritual people follow spiritual practices such as fasting and keeping vigil. By fasting, they overcame the desire of the body for food and by keeping vigil, they overcome its desire for sleep and rest. They preserve their spirit by keeping vigil in prayers and meditation, not settling for fasting in terms of its external act.

They deem it most important to bring the body into subjection that it may participate with the Spirit. They engage the body in the work of the Holy Spirit by doing prostrations so that the body may be as revering as the spirit in its submission to and praise of God. For man is both a spirit and a body. Subjecting the body also preserves one's chastity and purity. Those who follow the lusts of the flesh go by the wide gate, through the door of pleasure, about which Solomon said, "Whatever my eyes desired I did not keep from them" (Ecc. 2:10). This is the pleasure that spiritual people should reject, resisting unto bloodshed in the struggle against sin (Heb. 12:4).

What spiritual people also resist in order to submit the body is the pleasure of the senses. Even though the senses like to indulge in seeing, hearing, and tasting, the spiritual person should restrain and control them. In this struggle, he should not give rest to his body, but as the Apostle said, "And everyone who competes for the prize is temperate in all things" (1 Cor. 9:25). Self-discipline is entering through the narrow gate, for while a normal person works to please himself, a spiritual person keeps watch over himself, disciplining his body and bringing it into subjection. It is the same with his soul, he does not give in to its pleasure and desires.

The Apostle considered the lusts of the flesh to be love of the world (1 John 2:16) and love of the world to be enmity with God (James 4:4). Therefore, from the signs of walking in the narrow path is restraining the desires of the flesh, loving God, desiring His Kingdom, and presenting the body as an acceptable temple of the Holy Spirit (1 Cor. 6:19).

❊ Self-Denial ❊

The Lord Jesus Christ said, "If anyone desires to come after Me, let him deny himself, and take up his cross, and follow Me" (Matt. 16:24). He places God first, followed by the other, and last of all, himself. There is no doubt that self-denial is a narrow gate, for him to bear a slap on one cheek and turn the other also. And if someone compels him to walk one mile with him, to go an extra one. If someone wants to sue him and take away his tunic, to give him his cloak also (Matt. 5:39-41). If enduring wrongdoing and forgiving the one who has wronged you is difficult for many, how much more is loving one's enemies and doing good to those who hate you (Matt. 5:44). But the spiritual person needs to bear all things. He needs to give up many things and rise above the norm, despising himself for the sake of the Lord who said, "whoever loses his life for My sake will find it" (Matt. 16:25).

Certainly, this is not easy for a beginner on the spiritual path; it will be troublesome until he trains himself in perfect love. How true are the words of the scriptures, "We must through many tribulations enter the Kingdom of God" (Acts 14:22)! For it is necessary for the person who is walking the path of God to continually ascend the cross as the Lord said, "carry the cross and follow me."

St. Paul the Apostle also said about this, "I have been crucified with Christ; it is no longer I who live, but Christ lives in me" (Gal. 2:20). How deep is the phrase, "It is no longer I"? The only one who is able to say it is the one who has entered through the narrow gate, the one who has trained himself to disappear so that the Lord and other people may appear. He who is humble says, "It is no longer I..." He aspires to be last, to be the servant of all, and to take the last place, as St. Paul says, "in honor giving preference to one another" (Rom. 12:10). "It is no longer I" is said by the meek and humble person, for he is convinced that he is nothing.

No one can do this but the one who enters through the narrow gate. The one who does not value his opinion or "lean on his own understanding" (Prov. 3:5), preferring others to himself in everything and placing himself beneath everyone. He is not wise in his own opinion (Rom. 12:16) but blames himself to justify other people, bearing the sins of others that they may be innocent and he be guilty. In the depth of his love, he redeems all just as Christ did.

❈ Toiling for the Lord ❈

A spiritual person toils to fulfill the commandments, even if they seem difficult. He also toils for the sake of the comfort of others.

Take Moses the prophet, for example. It would have been very easy for him to remain in Pharaoh's house as a prince, indulging in luxury, wealth, and high rank. But he esteemed the reproach of Christ much richer than all the wealth in the storehouses of Pharaoh, "choosing rather to suffer affliction with the people of God than to enjoy the passing pleasures of sin" (Heb. 11:25). Moses toiled much, leading a stiff-necked people both as a prophet and a shepherd. He endured much complaining and disobedience from the people yet carried this burden with a compassionate heart that bears the sins of others.

Many prophets, ministers, and servants have toiled for the sake of the Lord. We venerate and honor them now; however, during their own time, they endured bitter tribulations. An example of this is St. Athanasius the Apostolic who defended the faith with power and deep understanding yet was once told, "The entire world is against you, Athanasius."

Another example is St. Paul who compared to the rest of the apostles was "in labors more abundant, in stripes above measure, in prisons more frequently, in deaths often... in weariness and toil, in sleeplessness often, in hunger and thirst, in fastings often, in cold and nakedness" (2 Cor. 11:23-27). This saint said about himself and his fellow servants, "But in all things we commend ourselves as ministers of God: in much patience, in tribulations, in needs, in distresses, in stripes, in imprisonments, in tumults, in labors, in sleeplessness, in fastings...by honor and dishonor, by evil report and good report" (2 Cor. 6:4-8) and "We are hard-pressed on every side, yet not crushed; we are perplexed, but not in despair; persecuted, but not forsaken; struck down, but not destroyed— always carrying about in the body the dying of the Lord Jesus" (2 Cor. 4:8-10). All believers face the difficulties of the narrow gate, regardless of their rank or status.

❈ The Narrow Path for All ❈

Even the most holy, the Theotokos Saint Mary, entered through the narrow gate. She lived as an orphan in poverty, gave birth to her son in a manger, and was estranged from her homeland. She bore much suffering when she saw her only Son being persecuted unjustly and crucified, even though He is the perfect and blameless One. The saying of Simeon the elder was fulfilled in her, "a sword will pierce through your own soul also" (Lk. 2:35).

In the same manner that the Holy Theotokos passed through tribulations, St. John the Beloved also experienced many hardships. He was imprisoned and whipped with the other disciples, and later was exiled.

All the martyrs and confessors passed through the narrow gate. For this reason, the Church venerates them above all the saints. For in their tortures and suffering, they confirmed their deep love for the Lord and so He rewarded them in the land of the living with a place that is indescribable.

❈ Evaluating Tribulation ❈

God does not forget any toil or effort that the believer exerts for His sake. He even says to the angel of the church of Ephesus who left his first love, "I know your works, your labor, your patience... you have persevered and have patience, and have labored for My name's sake and have not become weary" (Rev. 2:2, 3). The more a person toils on earth, the greater his reward will be in eternal life.

As the Apostle said, "For our light affliction, which is but for a moment, is working for us a far more exceeding and eternal weight of glory" (2 Cor. 4:17). He also said, "For I consider that the sufferings of this present time are not worthy to be compared with the glory which shall be revealed in us" (Rom. 8:18). For this reason, many people upon whom no tribulations came from the Lord would go out of their way to make their own gate narrow, struggling for His sake and for their spiritual work.

We should remember that the narrow gate is only narrow at the beginning, but then the spiritual person grows accustomed to it and finds spiritual pleasure in it.

CHAPTER 19

The Journey Towards Growth and Perfection

Some think that they have reached God when they abandon sin and walk in the spiritual path, but leaving sin only constitutes the negative struggle in the spiritual life. What, then, are the positive aspects? It is a long path, for spiritual life is never finished, but always grows and progresses.

Thus, a life of growth is one of the characteristics of the spiritual path. The Lord Christ liken it to "if a man should scatter seed on the ground, and should sleep by night and rise by day, and the seed should sprout and grow…first the blade, then the head, after that the full grain in the head" (Mark 4:26-28). He likened the spiritual person to a tree with continual and incessant growth. A tree grows in a calm manner, such that a person does not notice its growth on a daily basis but after an extended period of time. This quiet growth is likened to the righteous person: "The righteous shall flourish like a palm tree, He shall grow like a cedar in Lebanon" (Psa. 91:19).

A spiritual person grows in all aspects of spiritual life, in the knowledge and love of God, in purity, prayer, and contemplation. In fact, a person who does not grow is susceptible to lukewarmness and digressing. A car maintains its temperature as long as it is moving, but when it stops, its temperature ceases. Likewise, continuous journeying in the spiritual life inflames the heart, encompassing both one's relationship with God and other people.

In what direction does a person grow? He grows towards holiness as St. Paul said, "Just as He chose us in Him before the foundation of the world, that we should be holy and without blame before Him in love" (Eph. 1:4). Therefore, it is not merely a matter of repentance, but a life of holiness for the believer. St. Paul says in his last letter to the Philippians, which he wrote in Rome,

"Greet every saint in Christ Jesus...All the saints greet you, but especially those who are of Caesar's household" (Phil. 4:21,22).

Do you live out this holiness? Have you become a member in the community of the saints? Or do you continue to rise and fall, faltering between a life with God and life with the world? Holiness is not for a select few but is the goal of all. "Perfecting holiness in the fear of God" (2 Cor. 7:1) because "this is the will of God: your sanctification" (1 Thess. 4:3). In the Sermon on the Mount, purity of the heart was a condition to see God in eternal life. As He said, "Blessed are the pure in heart for they shall see God" (Matt. 5:8). Have you attained this holiness and purity, without which no one can see the Lord (Heb. 12:14)?

It is also important to note that holiness alone is not sufficient; a spiritual person must continue to grow in holiness until he reaches perfection. Relative perfection is what is meant by this because absolute perfection belongs to God alone. Relative perfection is the highest point of perfection that a person can possibly reach within their human limitations and what God has graced them with. About this perfection, the Lord said, "Therefore you shall be perfect just as your Father in heaven is perfect" (Matt. 5:48). Thus, it is necessary in your spiritual life to grow in holiness and purity until you reach perfection—the perfection of your ability and perfection of your life, that you may return once more to the original divine image in which God created you (Gen. 1:27).

But who is able to attain perfection? If you are unable to attain perfection, regardless of what you do and how much you struggle in your spiritual life, stand before God as a sinner. You struggle because you are asking for perfection while you are so far away from Him. This is why when the saints said about themselves that they are sinners, this was not some kind of an exaggeration or form of humility. Rather they felt that they had fallen short of the perfection that was asked by God. Given that perfection is limitless, spiritual growth was also limitless as well. An analogy of this is someone who is chasing the horizon. He stands and sees it far off at a distance connecting the earth and sky. He goes and sees it in front of him at the river. He goes and crosses the river, only to see that the horizon has extended to the mountains, and so on and so forth to no end.

Given that the matter is this way, contemplate the words of the Lord in the Gospel, "When you have done all these things which are commanded, say, 'We are unprofitable servants'" (Lk. 17:10). We have been given a lot of commandments in the Bible that we have not done until now. Even if we have kept all the commandments, it is our duty to say that we are unprofitable servants. "We have done what was our duty to do" (Lk. 17:10), and not continued in it unto perfection. Believe me, the level of "unprofitable" servants is a high one that you have not reached. There is no doubt that it is a long road and we have not taken a step towards it. We need to begin with a humble heart.

There is another verse in the Bible that I pause at. It is the saying of St. Paul in his letter to the Ephesians, "that you, being rooted and grounded in love, may be able to comprehend with all the saints what is the width and length and depth and height—to know the love of Christ which passes knowledge; that you may be filled with all the fullness of God" (Eph. 3:17-19). God knows that I continue to stop in front of this verse, bewildered and amazed, unable to reach anything from its wondrous depth. I will try to go back to the meditations of the fathers about it so that I may know. If I come to know anything, I will tell you because this is the work of the Spirit and not that of the mind or intellect.

This fullness, who is able to reach it? It is required of all of us, as St. Paul commands us in the same epistle, "Be filled with the Spirit" (Eph. 5:18). He says in another place, "Walk in the Spirit" (Gal. 5:16) and calls us to have the fruit of the Spirit (Gal. 5:22). There is a higher level that we need to reach in our growth to be filled with the Spirit. It is a long road that demands seriousness and dedication from a person to be able to walk it. One must first pass through repentance, purity, and holiness to be able to enter into the height and depth, to know the knowledge of Christ which is above all knowledge. He will move from walking in the

Spirit to bearing the fruit of the Spirit to being filled with the Spirit, to perfection. This is why we see St. Paul say, "Not that I have already attained or am already perfected; but that I may lay hold" (Phil. 3:12).

St. Paul—who was taken up to the third heaven, paradise (2 Cor. 12:4), who toiled more than the twelve apostles, traveled, preached, wrote 14 epistles, was imprisoned, tortured for the sake of the Lord, performed many signs, had many visions, spoke in more tongues than anyone—says after all that, "I have not counted myself to have apprehended; but one thing I do." We ask him, "What is this?" And he answers, "forgetting those things which are behind and reaching forward to those things which are ahead" (Phil. 3:13). He forgets all these superior gifts, all the toils in the service, being taken up to the third heaven, and moves towards his goal that he may attain it. What does he seek to attain? "the prize of the upward call of God in Christ Jesus" (Phil. 3:14). To attain this wondrous fullness. This is why he advises us, "Run in such a way that you may obtain it" (1 Cor. 9:24). He says with us, "I run thus" (1 Cor. 9:26). He also says, "Therefore let us, as many as are mature, have this mind" (Philippians 3:15).

Therefore, it is not a call just for the average person, but those who are perfect as well. It is a call for all to go towards this goal that they may attain it. We have all been called as children of God as St. John says, "Whoever has been born of God does not sin…and he cannot sin, because he has been born of God" (1 Jn. 3:9). He also says about this, "Whoever is born of God does not sin; but he who has been born of God keeps himself, and the wicked one does not touch him" (1 Jn. 5:18). Have you reached this level in which you cannot sin? This is a special level. It is not overcoming sin, struggling against it, and being victorious, but rather the level of a holy person who cannot sin. Who reached this state? I do not wish to only present to you the levels of the New Testament with all that it has in terms of richness and depth, but instead first take you to a commandment in the Old Testament, "You shall love the Lord your God with all your heart, with all your soul, and with all your strength" (Deut. 6:5). Who has been capable of loving God with all his heart? The word "all" points to the fact that there is nothing else in the heart, but God. There is no other love in the heart that competes with the love of God. This undoubtedly means a complete death to the world, emptying oneself and being full of the love of God.

Have you started on this path? Have you started with the fear of God which is the first step that leads to love? It is as the Scriptures say, "The fear of the Lord is the beginning of wisdom" (Prov. 9:10). The fear of the Lord means obeying Him and submitting to His commandments. In this way, you will reach God and enter into His Kingdom. The Scriptures say, "The Kingdom of God is within you." Do you feel that the Kingdom is within you? Have you started now to taste the Kingdom? Have you made it in your present life that you may enjoy the fullness of it in the life to come? Start with tasting the Kingdom. When you pray "Thy Kingdom come," ask that His Kingdom come upon your heart, mind, senses, body, and feelings. Then, you will sing and say, "The Lord has reigned" (Psa. 96:1).

You may ask after all this: What should I do as the road is long before me? It does not come with sadness, despair, or saying, "There is no use with me." These are all tricks from the devil trying to make you fall into having a low self-esteem so that you may stop struggling as a result of despair.

The most important piece of advice for you is this: The longest road starts with a single step. Start then by taking one step. Start with a step, no matter how small, weak, or lukewarm it is. Then, when God sees your desire in wanting to live a life with Him, He will help you. His grace will visit you, and His Holy Spirit's power will work within you. God Who worked in His saints is also able to work in you. The grace of God will not lead you to laziness, apathy, or negligence, but will work with you. In this way, you enter into communion with God and work for His Kingdom. His Kingdom is within you and as well as others. God is able to raise you up all at once as He did this with the penitent saints like Augustine, whom He moved from the depth of sin to the depth of meditation on divine matters with the depth of the love of God. Likewise, God took Mary of Egypt from blemish to monasticism as being one of the spirit-borne. She became one of the great saints!

If God wills for you to gradually progress in the spiritual life, His will be done. This is what happened with St. Moses the Black such that He gradually led him to repentance. He gradually granted him virtues, removed from him his hardness of heart, and granted him love for all people, wondrous meekness, and a transformative humility.

What is important, then, is to offer your heart to God so that God may fill it with His love. Tell Him, "Lord, I am unable to attain to Your love. There are other materialistic, worldly, and bodily loves that draw me, and I am weak before them. I ask that You grant me Your love as a free gift bestowed by You." As the apostle says, "because the love of God has been poured out in our hearts by the Holy Spirit Who was given to us" (Rom. 5:5).

Whatever you ask God to do for you, work also with Him in this. Be diligent and do whatever you are able to without an ounce of laziness in any spiritual matter. Open your heart so that God may fill it and be vigilant to not open your heart to the love of sin. Keep yourself away from anything that separates you from God. The little that you offer to God, He will accept as He did the two mites from the widow, and it will be precious in His sight. God knows your abilities and will not demand more than that of you. He will lead you step by step with His grace to wherever He wills. Therefore, do not look to the end and despair. Instead, look at this one step and consider how to take it properly. The more you are faithful in the little, God will entrust you with more according to His faithful promise.

❈ Obstacles to Growth ❈

We spoke in the last chapter about growth in the spiritual life, its necessity, and how it is a clear sign that one is walking properly in the spiritual path. We said that spiritual growth is a stage that leads to perfection. Now it is important for us to ask: Does every person grow spiritually? Does all spiritual growth continue and last?

What is clear is that spiritual growth is often stunted and delayed for many people. It stops at a certain stage and sometimes reverses backwards. What is the reason for all this? What are the obstacles to growth in the spiritual life? The obstacles are different for each person, but we will try to discuss some general ones.

The Envy of the Devil

The devil will not stand by idly if a person is constantly moving forward in his spiritual path, he will undoubtedly become an obstacle. This is sometimes called the envy of the devil, for demons envy those who progress in the love of God as they themselves have lost this beautiful relationship with Him and His Kingdom. For this reason, they fight not only spiritual growth, but spiritual life as a whole. It is written in the Wisdom of Sirach, "Son, when you apply yourself to the service of God, stand in justice and in fear, and prepare your soul for temptation" (Sir. 2:1). The Church reads this passage in the rite of the consecration of monastics because a person entering monastic life is trying to attain a life of perfection. The Church also reads this during the Third Hour of Holy Tuesday of the Holy Pascha, referring to the Lord Christ offering Himself to complete the great work of redemption and entering into the depths of temptation.

A spiritual person may oftentimes walk in the spiritual path with all his effort and all the grace he has received, victorious and growing spiritually. Others, however, are defeated by these wars, weakened, and unable to advance in their growth. When the devil saw that the work of salvation was about to be accomplished, he violently fought the disciples. So, the Lord Christ warned them saying, "Satan has asked for you, that he may sift you as wheat" (Luke 22:31). In this act of sifting, the growth of many disciples stopped and most of them digressed! Many saints and prophets also went through this sifting and warfare.

The devil does not leave anyone without fighting, so do not be upset if you face tribulations. Warfare is a characteristic of the spiritual path, and of the nature of the devil as well. Fight as much as are able to, but know that with every step that you ascend spiritually, a war will start to try to halt your growth. With every spiritual exercise that you practice, be assured if you experience a warfare, for if the devil were not afraid of this exercise, he would not fight you.

Warfare is one thing, falling is another. The stories of the desert fathers, the monks, and the anchorites are filled with spiritual warfare that was meant to prevent their growth, some succeeded and some failed. The devil is our enemy and will fight us in any case; however, he is not the only obstacle to spiritual growth, there are many helpers to him in this regard.

An Environment that Stunts Growth

A bad environment deters growth. A person must carefully choose his friends and companions, for they can obstruct his growth or cause him to digress. Just as a good friend can pull you up with him, a bad friend can pull you down, halting your growth. A husband who is not spiritual may hinder his wife's spirituality, and vice versa. For, marriage is participation in one life with a mutual agreement. If this agreement does not exist, spiritual growth can be delayed or, at minimum, lessened due to the surrounding environment.

Our father Abraham's growth was delayed for a time as a result of his environment. It was delayed when he was estranged in the land of Gerar, knowing that "the fear of God is not in this place"

(Gen. 20:11). Fear moved him to claim that Sarah was his sister, so Abimelech took her. In an environment that lacked the fear of God, the growth of this great prophet was not only stunted, but he also fell into sin.

The same thing happened to Lot the righteous in the city of Sodom. St. Peter said about this, "for the righteous man, dwelling them among them, tormented his righteous soul from day to day by seeing and hearing their lawless deeds" and he also said about him that he was "oppressed by the filthy conduct of the wicked" (2 Pet. 2:7, 8). Therefore, sinful surroundings and external pressures can delay even the growth of prophets and righteous people. Even if the righteous is victorious for a time, his righteous soul will be tormented "from day to day" by the surrounding pressures and his growth will cease.

In your spiritual pursuit, beware of befriending someone who may prevent or delay your growth. On the day that you take communion or confess, while in a good spiritual condition, be careful not to engage in a conversation that could blemish the purity of your mind and heart. For this reason, our fathers embraced solitude. They lived alone, away from all surroundings that could distract them or obstruct their growth, devoting themselves entirely to their spiritual work with God.

Likewise, all who love solitude—even those living in the world far from the wilderness—guard their solitude without wavering, without being spiritually fervent at one occasion then seeking other occasions that cool their fervency. In the Parable of the Sower, we hear about the thorns that choked the plants after they were fully grown (Matt. 13). Be vigilant, then, to keep away from all thorns that your spiritual plant may grow without being choked by the surrounding environment. In your growth, remember the words of the poet who said, "When can a building be complete, if you build up but another tears down"

Contentment

Another obstacle to growth is being content. This happens when a person reaches a certain spiritual level and no longer advances, believing he has attained ultimate spirituality. He does not think of progressing farther. Perhaps, the devil even makes him believe any further advancement is a form of extremism.

Our saintly fathers were never content with their spiritual lives; they were always striving to attain a better status. St. Paul who was taken up to the third heaven said, "one thing I do, forgetting those things which are behind and reaching forward to those things which are ahead" (Phil. 3:13). The one whose growth has stopped is susceptible to digressing backwards. For this reason, always try to grow, never be content with where you are.

Guarded by wisdom, place before you the high levels attained by the fathers that they may motivate you to struggle. Keep in mind this important principle: There is a big difference between growth and extremism. Wisdom is the balance between them, but the devil will use one principle instead of the other to try to trick you.

Erroneous Guidance

Another obstacle to growth is erroneous guidance. Erroneous guidance can stunt spiritual growth if the guide is not experienced in spiritual matters or is seeking personal gains. There are guides that are highly literal in their guidance, like the scribes and pharisees, of whom the Lord said, "If the blind leads the blind, both will fall into a ditch" (Matthew 15:14). For this reason, blessed is the person who is under wise, experienced guidance. It is important for
a person to "test all things and hold fast to what is good"
(1 Thess. 5:21). Do not heed the advice of everyone nor ask

anyone for guidance. As a poet once said, "Take knowledge from those who possess it and wisdom from the wise."

Imitation Without Discernment

What we mean by imitation is taking on another person's character without discernment. It is the literal imitation of the lives of saints or the practices mentioned in the *Paradise of the Fathers* without understanding what is appropriate for you. For each saint passed through many stages and trials before attaining the high spiritual level that was written about him in his hagiography. It is also the literal imitation of the words of the scripture or the life of your father of confession.

Each person has a distinct personality and a way of life that suits him spiritually and psychologically but may not be suitable for another person to imitate. A father of confession could be the one calling his spiritual children to imitate him, desiring to make them images of himself regardless of their personalities. This, however, obstructs their growth and spiritual advancement. Likewise, a father who enjoys a social life and gatherings could impede his son's spirituality if he forces him to adopt this lifestyle despite his love for calmness.

Pride

A person may be growing in his spiritual life, but at a certain stage, starts to compare himself to those lesser than him. As a result, his heart becomes prideful and his growth is halted due to this pride. Thus, the gifts of the Lord are only given to the humble. For a humble person, no matter how high of a spiritual state he attains, considers himself as nothing and compares himself to the higher levels of the saints, calling himself a sinner. The Lord then sees his humility and grants him more growth. Similarly, a person whose spiritual growth pleases him is content with his current state. He does not strive to reach a higher spiritual state, and so his growth stops.

We should avoid pride, not only because it stunts growth, but also because it causes one to fall. The Holy Scriptures say about this, "Pride goes before destruction and a haughty spirit before a fall" (Prov. 16:18). If you are walking in the spiritual path, beware lest you rise in your own eyes and fall into sin.

Another example of pride is a person who is visited by grace and raised up, yet attributes this rising to his own personal efforts and self-righteousness, not to the work of God. Grace thus abandons him, he becomes unable to rise a single step, and digresses. Perhaps in this case, the stunt of growth is a providence of grace.

Lack of Grace

Grace could leave a person not due to his own pride, but for fear that he might fall into the sin of pride. When grace is taken from him, he weakens and falls into many sins, like the great prophet Elijah. Elijah did not fear King Ahab nor the prophets of Baal but triumphed over them with great victory on Mount Carmel (1 Kings 18), yet he feared Jezebel (1 Kings 19:14). Similarly, David the prophet, upon whom the Spirit of the Lord descended, lived a life of prayer and psalms but later fell into some sins of beginners. Nevertheless, this helped him live a life of contrition and tears, showing us how growth can stop for a person's protection.

Administration

A person who leaves spiritual work and becomes involved in their administering is likely to be distracted from his salvation and that of others. Administration may cause him to fall into many sins that halt growth. Imagine if a monk living in solitude is taken and placed into a certain position or job!

Matters of administration are not bad in and of themselves, unless they become a reason that separates a person from his spiritual work and stops his growth. A priest who is successful in his spiritual work, but then takes on administrative matters in the church, can become distracted from his spiritual life. For this reason, many of our saintly fathers would escape positions to be able to devote themselves entirely to God. If any of you is distracted by administrative matters, he should ask himself: Has he continued to grow, or has he stopped and digressed?

Focusing on Outward Appearance of Virtues

Another reason for the stunt of growth is caring for the outward appearance of virtues. Some people care about growth in terms of quantity rather than in depth. They become concerned with the number of psalms they read rather than their spirituality while praying them, concerned with the number of metanias (prostrations) they make rather than their spiritual purpose. When they fast, they are concerned with the hours of abstinence and the amount and type of food rather than submission and giving the Spirit a chance to work. They are more concerned with the amount of prayer rather than the depth of it, the amount of reading rather than the depth of contemplation of what they read. Such people care about the outward appearance of virtues, not their depth. As for you, care more for the spirit, inner growth, and the hidden virtues.

Lack of Discernment

As Saint Antony the Great said, "the greatest virtue is discernment, having a good understanding of spiritual matters." How many people have failed spiritually because they did not understand the spiritual path well, did not have a wise spiritual guide and instead, depended on their own human efforts more than they depended on God and prayer!

Made in the USA
Coppell, TX
24 June 2022